MINISTRY OF SERVICE

MINISTRY OF SERVICE
A Manual for Social Involvement

by

Marie Schultejann, S.M.I.C.

PAULIST PRESS
New York/Ramsey/Toronto

Library of Congress
Catalog Card Number: 76-16901

ISBN: 0-8091-1967-6

Published by Paulist Press
Editorial Office: 1865 Broadway, N.Y., N.Y. 10023
Business Office: 400 Sette Drive, Paramus, N.J. 07652

Printed and bound in the
United States of America

Contents

Introduction

The United States Conference of Catholic Bishops in its pastoral message TO TEACH AS JESUS DID defined the total mission of the Church as (1) the proclamation of the Word, (2) the experience of community, and, (3) the ministry of service. Those engaged in parish administration or religious education were encouraged to evaluate their structures and curricula in the light of these goals and to make them effective tools in bringing the message of Christ to the people they served.

What had happened in American Catholic life, we might ask, to make this re-definition of Church mission an issue important enough to merit special attention by the Bishops? Hadn't the Church always concentrated on these essential channels of communication in spreading the Gospel message to the Christian community? Why at this moment in history did the Church speak?

Any casual survey of American Church history will immediately make it obvious that for over a century the teaching of the Word had been seen primarily to be a function of the parochial school system. Community was hopefully experienced in the two vital realms of the Christian family and in parish liturgical celebrations. However, something radical had happened in the area of service. Originally it was the family that cared for its own, providing its unique welfare system for the elderly, the ill and

1

the misfits. Gradually Church institutions sprang up and took in the outcasts of society providing them with the care that families could frequently not give. Today, however, we see that the ministry of service has shifted to the secular world. It is governments that meet the needs of the poor. The reasons for this transference of responsibility lay deeply imbedded in the changing nature of our modern society.

With the growth of technology, a multiplicity of social evils were spawned. Slums grew up in the rapidly expanding cities; new medical advances prolonged the lifespan of man with no corresponding provisions being made for the increasing number of aged; automation resulted in vast unemployment. Family and Church struggled to meet these rapidly expanding needs. Overwhelmed by their own increasing economic problems, people gradually began to accept the thrust of government into a limited form of social welfare. More and more government was called upon to assume the responsibility of caring for the elderly, the handicapped and the mentally ill. With this absorption of social service functions by secular society, the parish gradually evolved into a house of weekly worship. The charity, once an integral part of family and Church became secondary.

As the Christian community yielded its responsibility of service to the public sector of society, much of the sensitivity for persons and human suffering that characterized the approach of the family and Church was lost. Not infrequently did we hear of the "cancer in room 202" or the "schizophrenic in 405." Secular institutions, though more able to provide quality service from an economic standpoint, often lacked the spiritual dimension which alone makes it possible to penetrate the often repulsive exterior of disease and age recognizing the basic dignity of man. Today we witness a growing realization that a "value" has been lost and there are sincere efforts at many levels to recapture the ideal. "Personalism" in service and "the healing of the whole man" in medicine are goals toward which more and more committed people are working.

The love Christ taught was a one-to-one concern for others. He reached out and touched the person who was ill; he caressed the frightened child; he forgave the despairing sinner. We do not see him encouraging some vast enterprise to put his service on the assembly line. He taught us that love, if it is to heal radically, must be personal and authentic. It must spring from a heart that believes in the transforming power of love.

Many people today are eager to make a commitment that will improve the quality of life in our world but do not know where to begin. It is to these people, to the individual, to social action and service groups, to parish councils, and community organizations that this book is addressed. It is designed first of all to provide:

- ideas for service projects,
- a plan for organization,
- a list of resources that will provide necessary background and suggestions for effective service.

A secondary goal of this manual is to provide some basic ideas to those people who are more interested in finding solutions to the systemic problems that create the injustices in our society. We have

therefore included chapters on community organization and methods of influencing legislation as guides
toward producing radical change through social action.

Most of the service projects listed in this manual
can be instituted by anyone who is willing to set
aside a few hours a week. Social action requires
more of a commitment.

One of the most helpful tools in this manual will
be the list of resources. Most of these materials can
be obtained free of charge and will be found to be
extremely helpful.

I
Theology of Service

"In the beginning was the Word", and the Word was made flesh and dwelt among us". Christ, the Word, came to proclaim the Kingdom of God, a kingdom that was not of this world. It was a kingdom within the person, among persons, one that united us "Through him, with him and in him" to the Father. Relationships, not institutions were important.

Just as "God is Love", so too a person is made to the image and likeness of that love. (S)He is a spark of that divine flame that creatively works to renew the face of the earth. Love is the force that binds us together in the Spirit and commissions us to spend and be spent in making this love a living reality shared by all people.

Christ became one of us to bring us the "Good News"; we are saved, sanctified through his passion and death. We are made one with him and will rise again when we die. However, for many people in this world of human institutions and systems that breed injustice, the "Good News" is not evident. Many live as outcasts, as marginal persons in a society known for an affluence enjoyed only by a few. For reasons of economics, genetics, environment and age, they cannot find a place in this world that measures their worth by their money, productivity and power. What happens to the one who has made a mistake as a

5

youngster and is henceforth considered a criminal? (S)He cannot find a job and is condemned to poverty. What about the person diagnosed as emotionally disturbed or psychologically ill who finds that the wounds of early years have rendered him or her unable to cope with the world that we have built? What about the aged who exist on the fringes of society on a fixed pension that hardly guarantees them a decent life? All too many find themselves among the marginal persons who are not accepted, those who are ignored, unwanted. Yet, was not the "Good News" of salvation for all? Is his promise of eternal life so narrow that it embraces only the successful according to our standards?

Christ came, the Lord of History, the Lord of the Universe, and he gave us an example of service. In every page of Scripture we see him reaching out and touching the lives of the poor and rejected—healing them, loving them, saving them from their own despair. How often did he shock the elite by conversing with Samaritans, tax-collectors and adulterers. With him there were no marginal persons, only those who needed him. He came for the "lost sheep," those suffering in body and soul, and he taught us how to touch their lives with the healing salve of our compassion. Perhaps the sin from which we most need salvation is that of shutting out from our lives those who need us most.

Scripture, Old Testament and New, calls Christ the "suffering servant." This imagery is expressed at his Baptism (Mt. 3:17), at his transfiguration (Mt. 17:5), in his miracles (Mt. 17). Jesus is called the "Lamb of God," the servant of the Father who came to lay down his life for his sheep. St. Paul makes his atoning death the central feature of Christ's life (1 Cor.

15:3 and Phil. 2:7). By his example Christ came to establish the Kingdom. We are told to pray for that Kingdom of love and mercy in the words "Thy Kingdom come."

The people of God united in the Church he founded are also called upon to follow him in ministry to the poor, the needy, the rejected of society. They are asked to foreshadow "the Kingdom" by imitating Christ's example of service and unselfish love.

When we begin to love just a little, we are learning to die to ourselves, for every act of love is an emergence from our own selfishness. Dying does not come easily. As the Gospel tells us "it is a hard saying" and most of us do not want to hear it. Yet, unless we die, we cannot live in him for he tells us that it is in our willingness to lose our lives that we find him. A Christian is called upon to minister to all his fellow-persons, to give a drink of water to the thirsty, to wash the feet of others, to forgive seventy-times seventy. In a word, the real Christian mission is to learn to love as Christ has loved us.

All are called to ministry, but not all persons are fit for all kinds of service. There are functions within the "body of Christ" as St. Paul tells us that belong to those whom the Lord has called. Some have the gift of teaching; others, healing; still others of listening. Therefore, the following pages contain many types of service that can be initiated in order to bring the "Good News" to those who have often heard the Word, but who have only superficially experienced its saving quality in their lives. It is for each individual to listen to the interior voice of the Spirit and then hopefully to discern within these pages the particular service to which the Lord invites him or her to share in "here and now."

II
Building Blocks for Service

Societies throughout history have met the needs of the poor in a variety of ways. In primitive groups the extended family shared the care of the old and handicapped from birth until death through a pooling of labor and resources. With the growth of the nuclear family, various organizations including the Church and guilds took over the task of meeting the needs of those who could not care for themselves. As we enter the modern age, the trend has been to place people with similar problems into institutions in order to provide the maximum of care at a minimum cost. Institutionalization took the physically, mentally and emotionally needy out of the vision of the ordinary person; hence, it was easy to forget that they existed or that we had a personal responsibility toward them.

Need for Awareness

In visiting parishes that are in the process of setting up social action committees, we have often asked that members begin by making a list of needy people around them. Most people become perplexed and say: "Our parish has no problems." Pastors often agree. But, we ask, is it really that there are no problems, no suffering people, or is it rather that we have learned how to shut them out of our consciousness?

Acquiring an awareness of the many needy persons surrounding us is one of the primary efforts we are called upon to make. In this land of plenty, people go hungry; in our very neighborhood, old men and women long for friendship and a sense of worth; our schools are filled with children of immigrants who need extra help in the three "R's" to keep up with their classes; nursing homes are filled with people who are becoming senile long before their time because there is nothing to keep them functioning mentally. First and foremost, we need to look around us and recognize the countless people who reach out to us every day.

It is an extraordinary phenomenon that once our awareness of the problems of our society has been awakened, we go to the other extreme. A sense of despair overwhelms us. There seems to be no way in which we can respond to the multiplicity of needs, and we wonder where to begin. "Light a candle in the night and do not curse the darkness." Each of us can do something, no matter how small. Christ told us how. "Love one another." What can you do? First choose your area of interest.

Choosing a Program

The choice of a program is going to depend upon the interest and talents of the people who wish to become involved. It may be one person deciding on a plan of action, or a group who wants to work in a communal effort. Frequently it will be a parish committee or club that desires to find an avenue of service that will be meaningful to them. In any case, the first step is to make an honest appraisal of the talents and interests of those who wish to join in the project. What kind of time do they have available?

Does the majority prefer to work with adults or children? In the fields of education, recreation or social service?

Next, write for all the information about the types of service you wish to explore. At the end of each of the twenty suggested programs, and again in Chapter VII of this book, is a list of resources from which you can request material that will aid you in ascertaining the requirements in administration and operation of your area of interest. Ask yourself if you have people who can give the time required, or do you know where you can find such persons? Is there a money factor involved in your program. Can you find ways to subsidize it?

Once you have settled on the service that interests you, contact community service organizations that do similar work. They can help you by giving you advice on your program, supplying you with speakers to prepare you for better service, and in placing you in contact with persons to whom you can refer persons needing more professional help than your group is equipped to give.

For the individual wanting to become involved in an already established project, we suggest that you contact your nearest Volunteer Action Center or similar organization. After investigating your background and interests, their counselors will place you in a volunteer service near to your home in the area of your choice.

Looking for Leadership

There was a time when the laity waited for the clergy to telephone and ask for help. Women then served coffee at some parish meeting; men ran bingo. Today many of our laity desire to use their professional expertise to initiate meaningful service projects on their own. Leadership in this area can come from anyone with a minimum of organizational ability and a strong desire to fill a recognized need in the community. Anyone who has a few hours free while his or her children are in school can effectively organize and administer a program of helping others and do this right from his or her living room.

On the other hand, structures often help to create a powerhouse of human energy, and the parish is the source of many potentially active groups. Parish Councils, Social Action Committees, Legions of Mary, Rosary Societies, Holy Name groups and other Church organizations often look for projects that give witness to the faith they profess. Civic and community groups are also excellent reservoirs of leadership.

Who Wants to Help

You would be surprised at how many people want to use their free time profitably. "What can we do?" is a question that is heard frequently; few are prepared to give answers.

When a real need becomes clear, when it begins to pull on the heartstrings and consciousness of people within a community, you will find an amazing number of selfless people coming forward to help. Awareness is the key. People who will want to become involved can be found among:

- those whose children are in school several hours each day;
- those whose children are grown and who do not need to work;

- professionals who wish to make a contribution to society;
- those who have evenings or Saturdays free.

Here are some suggestions that will put you in contact with people who might want to help you with your program:

- Put an advertisement in your parish bulletin asking persons interested to contact you.
- Contact other churches, synagogues, etc.
- Ask each person who works with you to invite a friend.
- Write articles on your program for local newspapers and supermarket shoppers.

Need for Orientation

Venturing into anything new makes us feel insecure. Solution—find some professionals who will share their expertise with you and get you started. Most of them will be happy to offer their suggestions on a volunteer basis. Service projects directed toward enriching the lives of the suffering people in your community ordinarily do not need extensive training. You do not have to know clinical psychology to love children, nor geriatrics in order to comfort and befriend a lonely lady in your neighborhood. Love is the important element, and it heals most effectively when it flows naturally from a generous heart.

Getting the Program Off the Ground

The major elements in any successful program are thorough planning and good public relations. A well planned program with work properly delegated will have an excellent chance of success. Before embarking on your project, therefore, make a complete survey of problems you may encounter and the assets upon which you can draw. Don't overestimate the obstacles. Where there is a will, they can be surmounted.

You also have to convince people that what you are doing is of value. If you can create interest and enthusiasm in others, you will find that there will be replacements for dropouts. A variety of help will also come from unexpected sources. It has a snowballing effect.

Need for Credibility

In finding persons who need help, we frequently suggest that you contact Welfare Agencies, Hospitals and other service groups to get names. You may find a rightful hesitancy on the part of agencies and professionals to work with you unless you have the official backing of some reputable, established structure such as a Parish Council or Community Agency. It is a good practice to contact them personally and explain your plans. Ask them for suggestions to improve your program.

Screening

Not everyone wanting to work on a service program is necessarily fit to do so. In order to maintain your credibility in the community, it is necessary to screen carefully those who work with you on your project. Persons who are too aggressive, domineering, emotionally unstable or eccentric often do more harm than good. Ask persons in your sponsoring agency to suggest a plan for screening candidates for your particular service. (Cf. resources at the end of Chapter III. Any of the manuals for volunteer coordinators will contain excellent suggestions on screening.)

National Organizations

Some volunteer projects such as Big Sisters, Big Brothers, Friendly Visitors and others have state and national centers where a group can obtain valuable information. They also have set standards whereby the group can join the national organization if it wishes to do so.

However, no group should be deterred from a work it wishes to do by the standards of these groups. All too often because of our highly structured society we build more impersonal vehicles of service rather than stressing the QUALITY of compassion in the service we render. Professionalism has its place, but many times it is the warmth of a smile freely given, the hand clasp with a message, that heals most effectively.

Spanish-Speaking Programs

Many of the programs in this book are designed for the inner city where there is a growing Spanish population. They are often neglected because of the language barrier. Persons having a knowledge of Spanish could perform a needed service by organizing programs for these people.

III
Constructing a
Support System

In planning a program that will include a group of persons involved in some project, it is helpful to provide an effective support structure for those volunteering. Not all programs will need such an elaborate system as outlined below, but it can be tailored to your needs. A good support system should include:

- *Job Description:* a clear identification of areas where the volunteer is needed;
- *Orientation:* a plan for introducing the volunteer to his assignment;
- *In-Service Training:* to improve quality of volunteer work;
- *Supervision:* a person to whom the volunteer is responsible and can go for guidance;
- *Evaluation:* a record of the work of the volunteer;
- *Recognition:* a system of recognition of the service rendered.

Job Description

The preparation of a clearly written job description will help those joining your program to know what kind of a commitment is expected of them. Such a description might include:

15

- Job title: An interesting title can make the job attractive.
- Objectives: What are you trying to achieve by the project?
- Accountability: To whom is the volunteer accountable and what are the limits of this responsibility?
- Duties: What is expected of the volunteer?
- Qualifications: What kind of background should he possess in order to perform the task well?
- Evaluation: What criteria can be used for judging the success of the performance?

Orientation of Volunteer

Every volunteer task is performed in a certain setting under specific people. The volunteer needs to understand this environment and all the components of the institution where he will serve. A good orientation program can make him feel at home, and engender a spirit of cooperation.

Most organizations take the details of their structure for granted; volunteers need to be told what the staff already knows. Listed below are areas that should be included in your orientation when they apply:

- a history of the institution where the volunteer will serve;
- the administrative structure, who is in charge and who is responsible to whom;
- procedures and regulations that will effect the volunteer;
- an interpretation of duties, rights and responsibilities of the volunteer;

- a tour of the facilities;
- an introduction to the staff, particularly the immediate supervisor.

In-Service Training

When volunteer work is done by non-professionals in professional institutions there is often a feeling of insecurity. Persons willing to give their time often do not know how to tackle the problems encountered on the job. Since they are not being repaid in money, there is some obligation on the part of the institution to provide in-service training which will improve the quality of work rendered by the volunteer as well as to provide him with a learning opportunity. Sometimes it is sufficient for the supervisor to hold a personal interview at which time the volunteer can bring out his fears and frustrations. At other times, particularly when groups are serving in the same capacity, it is profitable to plan a workshop with specialists. The meeting might include a talk on some phase of the program and provide time for discussion. In this way the volunteer is encouraged to grow in knowledge on the job. An appraisal of the background and experience of each volunteer, as well as the nature of the assignment, will be necessary in structuring beneficial in-service programs.

Even with smaller parish programs, leaders are encouraged to offer opportunities to improve the quality of volunteer service. Qualified speakers are frequently willing to donate their time to this type of in-service training.

Supervision

The nature of supervision will depend on the type

of volunteer involvement. In institutional programs a coordinator of volunteers is usually appointed. It is the coordinator's task then to be available for consultation. It helps if the coordinator has a warm personality that can offer the necessary reassurance and support.

In smaller programs the supervision often falls to the leader of the program who must then assess the work of the volunteers. It is his or her duty then to provide direction as well as an evaluation of the work done.

Recognition

A simple "pat on the back" is still one of the best ways of upgrading the quality of work. The assurance that what we do is meaningful and appreciated often spurs us on to even greater sacrifice and effort. There are many ways of giving this recognition. Besides personal words of praise, a letter of appreciation is often enough to assure continued involvement. In other circumstances a pin or certificate for service rendered will provide the recognition that is needed.

Resources

Recruiting, Training and Motivating Volunteer Workers. Pilot Books, 347 Fifth Avenue, New York, New York 10016

The Volunteer Community: Creative Use of Human Resources. NTL Learning Resources Corporation, 2817 N. Door Avenue, Fairfax, Virginia 22030

Volunteer Coordinator Guide. University of Oregon,

Center of Leisure Studies, 1587 Agate Street, Eugene, Oregon 97403

A Manual of Directors of Volunteers. Los Angeles Volunteer Action Center, 621 South Virgil Avenue, Los Angeles, California 90005

Your Volunteer Program. Des Moines Area Community College, Project MOTIVATE, 2006 Ankeny Boulevard, Ankeny, Iowa 50012

Interviewer's Guide. (Helpful in Screening Volunteers) New York City Board of Education, School Volunteer Program, 20 West 40th Street, New York, New York 10018

Guidelines for Interviewers. Voluntary Action Center of New York City, Mayor's Office for Volunteers, 250 Broadway, New York, N.Y. 10007

Volunteer Recognition. National Center for Voluntary Action, Clearinghouse, 1785 Massachusetts Avenue, N.W., Washington, D.C. 20036

The following pamphlets can be obtained free from the National Center for Voluntary Action, Clearinghouse, 1785 Massachusetts Avenue, N.W., Washington, D.C. 20036.

Recruiting Volunteers
Recruiting Low-Income Volunteers
Everyone can Help Someone as a Volunteer
Wanted: Senior Volunteers
Looking into Volunteering?

IV
Ideas for Service

FRIENDLY VISITOR PROGRAM

Nursing Homes and Senior Citizen Residences are filled with people whose lives are spent in loneliness and isolation. Behind many a pretty curtained window in your neighborhood sits a little old man or woman whose family has passed away or whose children are living in other parts of the country. Who cares, they wonder, and yet they desperately want someone to care.

What Do Friendly Visitors Do?

A Friendly Visitor tries to give the older person a sense of worth by:

- creating a warm, friendly relationship;
- chatting about daily affairs and matters of mutual interest;
- writing letters, playing games, and reading aloud;
- emphasizing self-reliance, but giving assurance that help will be there if needed;
- listening;
- developing creative interests and hobbies.

Time Commitment

Normally only one hour a week is required. A person desiring to organize a Friendly Visitor Program could do so in about four hours a week. Most of the basic organization could be done by telephone.

Orientation

Nursing Homes will often work with you on planning an orientation program and will suggest where you can obtain speakers. A good preparation might include some or all of the following topics:

● The Friendly Visitor Program: What is it? (Social Worker)
● Physical Aspects of Growing Old (Nurse)
● Problems of the Handicapped   (Nurse)
● Psychological Problems in Aging   (Nurse or Psychologist)
● Community Resources for the Aged   (Welfare worker)
● The Joy of Service   (Priest, Minister, Rabbi)

Where to Look for Helpers

Since the time commitment is small and the hours flexible, many people in your community will be anxious to participate in a Friendly Visitor Program. Some may even want to involve their families. In your search for persons who might be interested in becoming a Friendly Visitor, try the following:

● In a short paragraph describe your program and ask your parish priest, minister or rabbi to publish it in your weekly bulletin.
● Write an article on your program for the local newspaper.
● Ask friends who are interested to ask another friend.

Where To Get the Names of Persons Who Want a Friendly Visitor

Some elderly people are very independent and would resent anyone coming into their home as a Friendly Visitor. Others want and need companionship. To find these persons:

● Contact social workers from hospitals for names.
● Contact Nursing Home Directors for people who would benefit from such a visit.
● Contact Activities Directors of Senior Residences.
● Ask your pastor and those of other faiths to give you names of people whom they know would appreciate a visit.
● Your articles in the local newspaper will often bring calls from people who want to make new friends.

Qualifications of a Friendly Visitor

Not every person is equally suited to work with the elderly. Qualities that help to form constructive and satisfying relationships with older persons are:

● a sense of respect and understanding for their problems,
● a sense of humor,
● patience,
● dependability,
● tactfulness: avoiding disturbing topics; keeping a positive thrust.

Agencies That Might Be Willing To Sponsor You

Social Action Committees

Parish Councils
Council on the Aging
Council of Churches
Social Service Agencies
American Red Cross

Resources

American Red Cross Friendly Visiting Manual. American Red Cross Volunteer Supportive Service, 23rd & Chestnut Streets, Philadelphia, Pa. 19103 (free)

Oregon's Basic Orientation Training Course for Volunteers Serving the Aged in Nursing Homes and Homes for Aged. Oregon State Health Division, Epidemology Division, Tuberculosis and Chronic Diseases Unit, P.O. Box 231, Portland, Oregon 97207 (free)

Oregon's Handbook for Volunteers Serving the Aged. (free—same address as above)

A Handbook for Friendly Visitors. Committee on Services to Older Persons, New Hampshire Social Welfare Council, Concord, New Hampshire (free)

Friendly Visitors. American Public Welfare Association, Chicago, Illinois (free)

TELEPHONE REASSURANCE

Many elderly persons live alone and need someone to check in on them occasionally. Many fear that they will become ill or perhaps die without anyone knowing their need. This program is designed to set up a system whereby interested persons telephone elderly persons each day to see that they are not in want. It provides psychological support by assuring them that help will be there if it is needed.

Time Commitment

That depends on you. You can make your telephone call long or short according to the time you have available.

Orientation

An orientation program is helpful but not absolutely necessary. The following talks would provide the volunteer with useful tools to do the task more effectively:

● The Telephone Reassurance Program: What Is It?
● The Physical and Psychological Aspects of Growing Old (Nurse)
● Proper Telephone Manner. (Telephone Company Resource Person)
● Resources Available to the Elderly (Welfare Worker or Social Worker)
● The Joy of Service (Priest, Minister or Rabbi)

Where to Get the Names of Persons to Be Called

Many of our sources will duplicate those found in the Friendly Visitor Program:

● Call welfare workers and ask them to inform you of people who need this kind of service.
● Contact Welfare Agencies and ask them to refer names to you.

- Get in touch with social workers at hospitals and ask them to let you know when persons who need this service leave the hospital.
- Ask your parish priest, minister or rabbi for names.

Agencies That Might Be Willing To Sponsor You

In addition to those agencies listed under the Friendly Visitor Program, you might also seek sponsorship from the Community Action for Social Affairs and the Jewish Family & Children Services.

Resources

Guidelines for A Telephone Reassurance Service. Superintendent of Documents, U.S. Government Printing Office, Washington, D.C. 20402. (Order No. GPO S/N 17 308:T 23)

Reassuring Calling Service. Reassurance Calling Service of Monmouth County, P.O. Box 323, Eatontown, New Jersey 07724 (free)

SOS-14. Establishing Telephone Reassurance Services. National Council on the Aging, 1828 L Street, N.W., Washington, D.C. 20036

Guidelines for the Development of a Telephone Reassurance Service. Community Planning Council of the Jacksonville Area, Inc. 505 North Main Street, Jacksonville, Florida 32202 (free)

Council Good Neighbors: Outreach Service for Older Adults. National Council of Jewish Women, 1 West 47th Street, New York, N.Y. 10036

NURSING HOME ACTIVITIES PROGRAM

Nursing Homes and Senior Residences are filled with countless persons who are unable to leave the premises. Their days and evenings are often spent in loneliness and monotonous routine. Many of these homes are required to have an activities director to initiate cultural, recreational and other projects that give these people an opportunity to come in contact with an expanded world. However, many of the programs are poorly organized and directors would often welcome outside volunteer help.

This project is designed to bring into Nursing Homes and Homes for the Aged a series of outside programs that can brighten up the lives of their residents. Basically it means scheduling programs—drama, music, dancing, etc.—that schools and clubs put on for other purposes.

Time Commitment

Most of the work of administration can be done by telephone or by letter. The time required will depend upon the magnitude of the program you initiate. Participation by others will be by assignment. They will be required to be present for the program scheduled and to act as coordinator between the school and the nursing home.

What Does the General Coordinator Do?

The General Coordinator takes the responsibility for the entire program and makes all assignments. (S)He

● Contacts the Activities Director of Nursing Homes and ascertains whether they would be interested in having schools conduct a program;

- Contacts schools and clubs and asks them for a commitment of one program during the year;
- Sets up a schedule and coordinates it with the school and home;
- Appoints a member of the committee to coordinate the program when it takes place.

What Do the Coordinators Do?

The local coordinator is responsible for one program at a specified location. It is his or her duty to:

- Call the Nursing Home early in the week to see that the program can occur as scheduled.
- Call the school and find out what time the students will arrive, and how long the program will last.
- Be on site early to solve any last minute problems. In this area public relations are most important. The staff may already consider the movement of the patients to one general location an inconvenience. Any added inconvenience would make them hesitant about scheduling future programs.
- Write letters of thanks to both the schools and the homes for their participation and cooperation in the program.

Orientation

Persons involved in this program need only a short orientation on the purposes of the effort. It might include:

- an explanation of the problems of the elderly and

their need for challenging experiences *(Person trained in geriatrics)*;
- an evaluation of the problems encountered by the staff of a Nursing Home in cooperating with the program *(Member of a Nursing Home staff)*;
- a quick survey of possible things that might be done as activities *(An Activities Director of a Nursing Home)*.

Qualifications

Good public relations are essential in this work. Desired qualities would include:

- a gentle, non-threatening manner in dealing with schools and Nursing Home personnel;
- an understanding of the problems involved in the movement of patients and the change of routine in Nursing Homes;
- a patience and perseverence that will not give up at obstacles.

Agencies that Might Sponsor Your Group

Council on the Aging
Council of Churches
Social Action Committees
Parish Councils

Resources

Recreation in Nursing Homes. National Recreation & Park Association, 1601 North Kent Street, Arlington, Virginia 22209

Dance Therapy Program for Nursing Homes (Hand Dances). Unitarian Universalist Women's Federation, 25 Beacon Street, Boston, Massachusetts 02108

Oregon's Basic Orientation Training Course for Volunteers Serving the Aged in Nursing Homes and Homes for the Aged. Oregon State Health Division, Epidemiology Section, Tuberculosis and Chronic Diseases Unit, P.O. Box 231, Portland, Oregon 97207 (free)

Oregon's Booklet, Being a Trained Volunteer in Nursing Homes. (Same address as above. free)

Manual on Volunteer Services in Homes for the Aging and Nursing Homes. Texas Association of Homes for the Aging, P.O. Box 4553, Austin, Texas 78765

Volunteer Service Corps Handbook. American Nursing Home Association. 1025 Connecticut Avenue, N.W., Washington, D.C. 20036

Be a HEP. National Center for Voluntary Action, Clearinghouse, 1785 Massachusetts Avenue, N.W., Washington, D.C. 20036

HOSPITAL FOLLOW-UP

Social workers tell us that many people leave the hospital too weak to care for themselves. Often they cannot afford a private nurse or housekeeper to care for them until their strength returns. It is for these people that this program is designed.

Time Required

Even one hour given generously can be a tremendous service.

Services the Volunteers Can Offer

People recuperating from a serious illness or operation often need the following services:

● visits to see that they are not in want,
● preparation of a meal,
● housecleaning chores,
● shopping or banking trips,
● referral to other agencies that might meet the persons' needs on a more continued basis.

Orientation

No formalized training program is needed. However, if a group is involved, the coordinator of the program could arrange talks in the following areas:

● Physical and Psychological aspects of Illness (Nurse)
● A First Aid Course (Volunteer Ambulance Service)
● Referral Services (Welfare Department)

Qualifications

No special qualifications are necessary. You will need a willingness to be of service, patience and an understanding of illness.

Where do you find people who need help?

Contact social workers in hospitals and your welfare department. These people come in contact with people who will need the follow-up service.

Resources

Volunteer Service. Association of Volunteer Bureaus, United Community Funds and Councils of America, New York, N.Y.

Welfare Services Through the Use of Volunteers. American Public Welfare Association, Chicago, Ill.

Servicing Crippled Children and Adults. National Society for Crippled Children and Adults. National Society, Chicago, Ill.

A Handbook for Volunteers. Kansas State Department of Social Division of Services for the Aging, Topeka, Kansas.

The Organization & Operation of an Information, Referral & Follow-up Program. National Easter Seal Society, 2023 West Ogdon Avenue, Chicago, Illinois 60612

Focus on Active Listening and Referral. Housing Listening Post, State Office of Volunteer Programs, 701 Dayton Street, Edmonds, Washington 98020 (free)

Reaching Out to the Isolated Aged. Hemp Street Settlement, Urban Life Center, 265 Henry Street, New York, N.Y. 10002 (free)

Volunteer Services for Older Persons. National Center for Voluntary Action, 1785 Massachusetts Avenue, N.W., Washington, D.C. 20036 (free)

What Are You? I Am Old. State Communities Aid Association, 105 East 22nd Street, New York, N.Y. 10010

LITURGICAL COORDINATORS
IN NURSING HOMES
AND SENIOR CITIZEN RESIDENCES

Many Nursing Homes and Senior Citizen Residences have no religious services scheduled because of the lack of personnel to coordinate such programs. A Liturgical Committee would be helpful in planning to bring the comforts that religion can offer to Protestants, Catholics and Jews within these homes.

Time Required

Again, much of the work can be done from your home telephone. However, in the initial stages of organization, leaders should personally visit key people in nursing homes or senior residences and establish a willingness to accept these services. Members of the clergy of all faiths should also be contacted to ascertain their availability.

What Would the Liturgical Committee Do?

- Establish contact and a working relationship with a home that needs this service.
- Work out a schedule for regular religious services at a convenient time.
- Contact priests, ministers and rabbis who would be willing to serve in the program and ascertain if the time they have available can fit into the schedule of the home.
- Find out what preparations will be needed for each service and what kind of facilities are required.

- Check on the length of the service.
- Appoint a member of the Liturgical Committee to make these preparations for the service and attend the service so that further requests can be met.
- Coordinate the program with the home so that resident members of the various faiths will be informed of the service and can make a request to attend.

Qualifications

The coordinator of this program needs tact and good public relations. (S)He must have an ability to work with people and the sensitivity to pick up potential problems before they reach the crisis stage. Furthermore, the coordinator will need:

- *Organizational Ability.* A program such as this can sometimes be viewed by the home as an inconvenience since it requires extra work on the part of the personnel to bring the patients to the liturgical function. If the program is well coordinated, much of the frustration of the staff can be eliminated.
- *Availability.* Some member of the committee must be present for the services.
- Understanding of the problems and isolation of the aged and ill.

Orientation

A well-planned orientation program such as the following would help to eliminate many of the potential problems that can occur:

- Organization and Operation of the Nursing Home or Senior Residence.
- The Importance of Religion in the Lives of Men and Women.
- The Physiological and Psychological Effects of Illness and Old Age.
- Preparation for a Catholic Liturgy, a Protestant Service and a Jewish Service.

Resources

Eucharistic Liturgies. Gallen, S.J. New Jersey. Paulist Press.

Home Celebrations. Lawrence E. Moser, S.J. New Jersey: Newman Press.

Rite of Anointing & Pastoral Care of the Sick. Catholic Book Publishing Company.

Communal Anointing of the Sick. Calkins. Chicago: Claretian Publishing Company.

How To Prepare Mass. Michael Gillian, Oak Park, Illinois: Catholic Press.

Rediscovering Ritual. Paul D. Jones. Paramus: Newman Press.

PEN PALS

For many, loneliness is an integral part of growing old. Our society often abandons the elderly. Their final years that should have been joyful years of sharing the wisdom accumulated with age are often spent passively waiting for death. Their hours drag because of the few outside contacts available to them.

Youth has a tremendous power to bring light and life into the lives of the elderly. This project can be organized by a housewife or teacher who is interested in involving youth in service to others. It involves having children adopt an older or ill person by writing to them about their "fun and games". These letters hopefully will ripen into friendship and visits, but the immediate purpose is to encourage pen-pals.

Time

Flexible. Use contact with youngsters that you already have. This is an excellent project for a girl scout troop or similar group.

Qualifications

All you need is a desire and ability to motivate the young and to understand the needs of the elderly.

How Do You Get Names of Persons Who Would Benefit from Letters?

There are certain key people who will be happy to give you names. Contact:

- priests, ministers, rabbis for names of people whom they meet on their pastoral work,
- welfare social workers,
- hospital social workers,
- activities directors of Nursing Homes and Senior Citizen Residences.

Orientation of Children

You will first of all need a vehicle for motivating

the children on an on-going basis, so form a club.

- Talk about the loneliness of many people in our society and what they could do about it.
- Give hints on what to write in letters.
- Tell them what a letter can mean in the life of an older person.

The club might meet once a month to:

- share the experiences of the children,
- accept and orient new members,
- check up on the fidelity in writing,
- stimulate continued enthusiasm.

Resources

(See resources for Friendly Visitors, and Hospital Follow-up)
Letter-writing. Watson, & Eickler. Englewood Cliffs: Prentice Hall.

DIAL A DRIVER

The elderly and handicapped often need drivers to take them to the hospital for tests, the doctor's office, the bank or shopping. This program is designed to offer this assistance by organizing a group of volunteer drivers who will be able to make one trip a week. Housewives, retired men and women, and teenagers can participate in this program according to the time they have available. Trips are scheduled for convenience as to time and geographical location. Drivers supply their own car and gasoline.

How to Get Started

- Get a list of persons willing to drive one day a week and the times they are available.
- Write an article for your newspaper telling about the service you wish to extend.
- Contact social workers in hospitals and your welfare department offering them your service.
- Inform your priests, ministers and rabbis that you have this service organized.

Information the Driver Needs to Do the Job

- the name and address of the patient whom he will drive;
- the name and address of the hospital, doctor or clinic and the name of the social worker who is working with the patient;
- the date, and time of the appointment.
- If the patient will be accompanied by someone, the driver should be informed.

Orientation

When working with the ill or elderly, many emergencies can occur. The better prepared the drivers are to meet these emergencies the more successful your program will be. A good orientation program might include the following:

- a first aid course from your local First Aid Squad;

- talk on conversational techniques in dealing with the ill; any social worker could give you valuable tips in this area.
- information on appropriate insurance coverage and income tax deductions acceptable for driving for charitable purposes.

Qualifications for Participation in the Program

- a driver's license,
- at least two years' driving experience,
- patience and tact,
- an available car,
- a sense of humor.

Resources

Wheels, Inc. Information Kit. A Transportation Program for the Ill. National Center for Voluntary Action, Clearinghouse, 1735 Eye Street, N.W. Washington, D.C. 20006 (free)

Transportation Programs and the Volunteer. National Center for Voluntary Action, Clearinghouse, 1735 Eye Street. N.W. Washington, D.C. 20006 (free)

An Outline and Suggested Methodology for New Transportation Programs. Progress on Wheels, Charles A. Tarse, 129 Mansfield, St. Belvedere, N.J. 07823 (free).

Project Helping Wheels, Superintendent of Documents, U.S. Government Printing Office, Washington, D.C. 20402. (Order Number: GPO SD 1762-00078)

BIG-BROTHER/BIG-SISTER PROGRAMS

There is a tremendous need for adults who will assist young persons in growing up, particularly when they have been deprived of healthy home relationships. Children in homes for juvenile delinquents, mentally retarded, the emotionally disturbed—all need someone who really cares about them as a person.

There are national organizations with high standards for both big-brother and big-sister programs. Whether you join these national groups or work on an individual basis, you can learn much from their experience and the materials they have available.

It would seem that the need for committed persons to guide youth is much greater than the number of adequately trained people available at the present time. There appears to be a need for mature persons who can offer assistance on a less structured basis.

Time required

Most organizations engaged in this work require two hours per week. Organization of such a program would require considerable time.

Leadership

Ideally, leadership of a big-brother or sister program should come from someone educated in social work or some branch of psychology. The matching of an adult with a child requires professional expertise. Also, it is necessary to screen out from this program persons who are not emotionally equipped to work effectively.

What Do Big Brothers/Sisters Do?

- offer companionship and understanding to a growing boy or girl who has little support from home,
- promote growth and development through friendship,
- share cultural experiences and home life with youngsters.

Who Can be a Little Brother/Sister?

- any fatherless boy or motherless girl aged eight through seventeen who needs friendship and affection. Some are:
  emotionally deprived
  isolated in an institution
  in trouble with the law

How to Get Names of Little Brothers / Sisters

First you will need to establish your credibility with people who will give you names. Schools, courts, social agencies, social workers and churches know many children needing this kind of service.

Qualifications

- responsibility and maturity,
- emotional stability,
- understanding of youth and their problems,
- a non-judgmental attitude.

Agencies That you can Contact

Big Brothers of America

Big Sisters Association of Rhode Island
Parish Councils
Probation Courts
Institutions for mentally retarded, emotionally disturbed or handicapped children.

Resources

Big Brother Program Materials. Big Brothers of America, 341 Suburban Station Building, Philadelphia, Pa. 19103 (free)

Handbook on Organization and Policies: Big Sisters Association of Rhode Island. Big Sister Association of Rhode Island, Operational Division of Family Services, Inc. 333 Grotto Ave., Providence, Rhode Island 02906 (free)

Big Brother/Big Sister Program. Office of Volunteer Community Service, University of Virginia, 1908-Lewis Mountain Road, Charlottesville, Virginia 22903 (.25¢)

Everything You Wanted to Know About the Big Brother/Big Sister Volunteer Program. Eugene Public Schools School Aids Program, 200 North Monroe, Eugene, Oregon 97402 (free)

What It Means To Be A Little Brother or Sister (Same address as above-free)

People to People Volunteering. (Same address as above-free)

Volunteers Help Youth. National Center for Voluntary Action, 1785 Massachusetts Avenue, N.W., Washington, D.C. 20036

Home Care, Proctor & Gamble Company, Supervisor Educational Services, P.O. Box 599, Cincinnati, Ohio 45201 (free)

RECREATIONAL ASSISTANT
IN A CHILDREN'S HOME

Within your area there are no doubt homes for emotionally disturbed children, the handicapped, the mentally retarded and others. Each of these homes has a need to bring outsiders into their program in order to give relief to the staff and expose the children to new personalities. Groups or individuals that are willing to come on a regular basis are usually welcome.

The program involves either recreational or tutorial work. Both are needed. Persons equipped in either of these areas can find an outlet for their creative talents. There is also a place for persons who can merely build up good relationships with these children.

How to Get Involved

● Get a group together, or if you wish, apply alone. Contact the home and set up an appointment for an interview.
● Be ready to tell the director of the home what your qualifications and interests are.
● Be prepared to offer specific time slots when you can be available.

Orientation

When working in professional institutions, the institution itself usually provides the training necessary to do the job. If nothing is scheduled and you feel the need for information that would equip you to function more efficiently on the job, ask the director to set up a workshop if more than one volunteer is involved. Otherwise ask for a supervisor to whom you can go with your questions.

Qualifications

The most basic of all qualifications for successful work in this area is a sincere love for children. You will also need:

- Patience. Working with certain types of children can at times be difficult.
- Dependability. It is important for the children to know that you care enough about them to be there regularly. Failure to attend is often interpreted as rejection.
- A willingness to learn. Most volunteers can benefit from the advice of the professionals on the staff.

What Kind of Work Would You Do?

The tasks you may be asked to do vary. Children need:

- help in writing letters,
- someone to initiate games with them,
- chaperons on trips,
- someone to listen to their problems,
- music lessons, sewing, knitting, handicrafts, etc.,
- tutorial help in math, reading and writing.

Resources

Recreation for Special Populations and *Recreation for Disabled Children*. National Recreation and Park Association, 1601 North Kent Street, Arlington, Virginia. 22209

Recreation for Autistic and Emotionally Disturbed Children. National Institute of Mental Health, Citizen Participation Branch, Parklawn Building, 5600 Fishers Lane, Rockville, Maryland, 20852.

The Playground Summer Series. National Recreation and Park Association, 1601 N. Kent Street, Arlington, Virginia. 22209

The Tutor's Handbook. Voluntary Resources Division, United Planning Organization, 1021 Fourteenth Street. N.W., Washington, D.C. 20005 (free)

More Tutoring Clues. (Same as above and free)

For the Tutor: Tutor's Grab Bag. National Commission on Resources for Youth, 36 West 44th Street, New York, N.Y. 10036 (free)

POLICEMAN'S PARTNER

This program originated in the Midwest where policemen agreed to participate in a school program designed to improve relations between the police department and the young adult. High school students were permitted to enroll in a program which required them to spend 100 hours in a patrol car or with the officer at the desk. At the end of a year of experimentation, crime in the school had lessened 85%, attendance at school increased 75% and the student's quality point index rose 5%. Waiting lists of over 100 students attested to the program's acceptance by the students.

Leadership for this project must come from the faculty of the high schools or from the members of the police department.

What Do Students Enrolled in this Program Do?

- They ride with the policeman as he patrols his assigned areas.
- They learn from him the procedures that he uses in combating crime.
- They assist the man at the department desk in taking and transferring calls.
- They receive ½ credit from their high schools for their commitment of 100 hours.

Orientation

The students receive on-the-job training. However, it might be helpful to have an orientation program for the policemen participating in the program in order to provide:

- an understanding of the goals of the program,
- a method of evaluating the work of the student who will need records for the school,
- a plan for coordinating the work of the school with the police department.

Qualifications of Policemen

- Honesty. The example received from the policeman is vital to the student's growth.
- Willingness to participate. A man who does not understand the younger generation cannot work successfully with them.
- Faith in the goals of the program.

Resources

Mr. John Graves, Franklin High School. 3100 Joy
Road, Livonia, Michigan. 48150. (Originator of
the Program)

*Citizens Action to Control Crime and Delinquency:
Fifty Projects.* National Council on Crime and
Delinquency. Continental Plaza, 411 Hackensack
Avenue, Hackensack, New Jersey 07601 (free).

HELP! Stop Crime. Governors Crime Prevention
Committee, Governor's Council on Criminal Justice, Post Office, Drawer 3786. Tallahassee, Florida. 32303. (free)

*Cues for Action: Twenty-Two Steps to Safer Neigh-
borhoods.* National Alliance for Safer Cities,
Nancy Mamis, Executive Director, 165 East 56th
Street, New York, N.Y. 10022 (free)

Helping Youth. Superintendent of Documents, U.S.
Government Printing Office, Washington, D.C.
20402

WELCOME TO OUR TOWN

We live in a mobile society and most of us have
experienced the frustration of moving lock, stock
and barrel into a new home. Remember the unfor-
gettable experience of those first few days living
among boxes and cartons, trying to set up a simple
form of housekeeping, or finding a place to sleep
until some order could again be brought into our existence? It was a time when "a helping hand" would
have been appreciated.

This program is designed to find out when new people will be moving into an area, and to plan a community effort to assist them in getting settled.

Time Required

Flexible.

How to Get Started

Get a committee together of persons who would like to become involved in this project. Then:

- Ask real estate offices if they will inform you when families will be moving into your area.
- Gather a group of friends who will make themselves available when the newcomers arrive.
- Formulate a group plan of providing a meal for them on the day their moving van arrives.
- From there on, think creatively. There are so many ways in which you can be of help.

Qualifications

You need a sincere desire to be of service. This will come through even to strangers who may be embarrassed at first by your offer to help.

Orientation

If you have personally had the experience of moving, that experience will be your best orientation. You will have empathy.

Agencies that Can Help You

If there is a Welcome Wagon in your town, join them. There is no need to duplicate services. Organizations that have been in operation for some time have the "know-how" for better service. If you are some distance from a center, ask to set up a branch under their direction. Other organizations that might help you are:

● Parish Councils,
● Social Action Committees,
● Women's Junior League,
● Council of Churches.

Resources

Guidelines for the Volunteer Coordinator. Betty Wiser, 404 Dixie Trail, Raleigh, North Carolina 27607
A Manual for Directors of Volunteers. Los Angeles Voluntary Action Center, 621 South Virgil Avenue, Los Angeles, California. 90005
Volunteer Clearing House Operating Manual. Volunteer Clearing House, 114 B Kansas Union, University of Kansas, Lawrence, Kansas 66145 (free)

NEIGHBORHOOD BOOK AND MAGAZINE EXCHANGE

With the rising cost of living it is often difficult to afford all the magazines and books that one would like to read. Why not organize a club to exchange these "mind expanding" tools for growth. The program is designed to provide a broader spectrum of reading material for all age groups on a regular basis through neighborhood exchange.

Time commitment

Minimal organizational time.

How to Set up the Program

- Ask four or more neighbors to meet with you if they are interested in a regular exchange of reading materials.
- Sit down together and agree on what magazines you would all like to have, but can't afford.
- Draw up a list of book clubs that offer good selections.
- Divide the chosen items among the group so that each family has approximately an equal financial commitment.
- Decide on a regular policy of exchange. (Every Friday one of the children can make the rounds and exchange the material)

Criteria for Success

This program requires discipline from its members. There must be a willingness to put oneself on a time schedule for the use of books and magazines. Provisions should be made in the policies of the club that a member may have the book returned to him if he has not completed it.

ALTERNATIVE PLAN: FORM A PARISH LIBRARY

Many parishes begin a library where people can come at specific hours to pick up books and magazines. This program involves a greater time commitment and more organization than the one above, but is a very valuable service to the parish or community.

Organization

- Gather a group that would like to sponsor a parish library.
- Form committees for staffing library at regular hours, cataloguing, etc., choosing and ordering books.
- Find facilities where library can be set up.
- Conduct a book drive in the parish in order to get a good start at minimum cost.
- Formulate definite policies for the use of the library.
- Hold an open house when you are ready to begin.

Leadership

It will be helpful if one person on the committee has some experience or background in library science. However, sufficient competence in operating a parish library can be supplied by a visiting professional librarian who would be willing to work with you on a consultant basis. Contact your school or community libraries and ask for the help you need.

Resources

Effective Library Exhibits, Kate Coplan, New York: Oceana Publications.
An Introduction to Librarianship. Edmund Corbett. London: Clark Publication.

Guide to the Use of Books & Libraries. Jean Key Gates. New York: McGraw Hill.
The Vertical File. Shirley Miller, Littleton; Librarians Unlimited.

CULTURAL ENRICHMENT

When we speak of service programs we often do not realize that providing cultural advantages to children is a very important contribution to helping them grow. Not only must a child learn to read and write, but he must also be exposed to drama, music, art and the finer experiences of life.

A small group of interested women with a little time on their hands could easily set up a cultural enrichment program for the children of their neighborhood, for a school in a deprived area, or for a children's home. Speakers, dance and song groups, drama clubs are often willing to present their arts either on a volunteer basis or at a minimum cost.

Time Requirement

This type of program requires a considerable amount of time. It needs people who are dedicated to the service.

How to Set Up a Program

● Gather a group of interested persons who believe that there is a vital need for cultural opportunities in the neighborhood.
● Discuss and settle on the type of program you think would have the most appeal.

- Decide on what age group you wish to reach.
- Set up a definite schedule, time, dates and possibilities.
- Contact fine arts departments on college campuses, local art groups and ascertain their fees and availability.
- Locate facilities where your program can be conducted.

Ventures You May Want to Consider

- Bus trips to historical sites
- Lectures
- Plays
- Musicals
- Art shows
- Movies
- Visits to museums
- Field trips to parks in which you live close to nature

Qualifications

- creativity and organizational ability,
- good public relations.

Alternative

Getting the children involved in a program of their own making is usually the best way to promote the arts. Let the children plan their own art show, poetry contest, write and produce their own play, put on a concert. The child who actually participates in any art form is learning something of immense value. You may be fortunate to find a high school or elementary school teacher in your area who would be willing to work with you on this project.

Resources

Picture Talks on Art. Rice Museum, Rice University. Institute for the Arts, P.O. Box 1892, Houston, Texas. 77001. (free)

Music is Fun for Children. Play Schools Association, Inc. 120 West 57th Street, New York, N.Y. 10019

The Design Game, (Kit) University of Illinois, 171 Krannert Art Museum, Champaign, Illinois 61820

Ethnic Art Slide Library Catalog, Ethnic American Art Slide Library, The College of Arts and Sciences, The University of South Alabama, Mobile, Alabama 36688. (Minimal cost)

Media Handbook for the Arts, Mid-American Arts Alliance, Systems Building, Suite 233, 3835 Holdrege, Lincoln, Nebraska 68503

Traveling Exhibits, Traveling Exhibits Service, Smithsonian Institute, Washington, D.C. 20560 (Write for information)

Playscapes Association for Childhood Education. International 3615 Wisconsin Avenue, N.W., Washington, D.C. 20016

Songs Children Like. 3615 Wisconsin Avenue, N.W., Washington, D.C. 20016

Games Enjoyed by Children Around the World. 3615 Wisconsin Avenue, N.W., Washington, D.C. 20016

Creative Dramatics for All Children. 3615 Wisconsin Avenue, N.W., Washington, D.C. 20016.

How to Run a Children's Musical Theater. San Jose
  Children's Musical Theater, 4735 Camden Avenue, San Jose, California 95124

TUTORIAL PROGRAM

Many children do poorly in school because they
lack the basic skills of reading, writing and arithmet-
ic. Because of this handicap many children who have
above-average ability, never achieve. Slow learners
and children of immigrant groups are two specific
groups that frequently need tutorial help.

Time Requirement

Involvement in a tutorial program usually requires
a commitment of about three hours twice a week.

Orientation

Schools will frequently offer a basic training program for tutorial volunteers which will include methods of teaching remedial reading or basic mathemat-
ics. Check this out at the school to which you
volunteer.

Qualifications

- patience,
- an understanding and love of children,
- some basic knowledge of how to teach reading,
  writing or math,
- an ability to relate to the age group you are tutoring,

• an ability to inspire confidence.

What Does a Tutor Do?

• attends school at least three times a week and offers his assistance for the slow student;
• works with the student on a one-to-one basis;
• tries to inspire self-confidence in the student who has lost faith in his powers to achieve·

Resources

The Tutor's Handbook, Voluntary Resources Division, United Planning Organization, 1021 Fourteenth St., N.W., Washington, D.C. 20005 (free)

More Tutoring Clues. (Same address as above-Free)

For the Tutor: Tutor's Grab Bag. National Commission on Resources. 36 West 44th Street, New York, N.Y. 10036 (free)

Tutoring Tricks and Tips. National Commission on Resources, 36 West 44th Street, New York, N.Y. 10036 (free)

Tutor Handbook for Volunteers in Public Schools. Tutorial & Volunteer Services, Cincinnati Public Schools, Education Center, 230 East Ninth Street, Cincinnati, Ohio 45202

Guidelines for the Volunteer Tutor. Des Moines Area Community College, PROJECT MOTIVATE, 2006 Ankeny Boulevard, Ankeny, Iowa, 50012

CLOTHING FOR THE POOR

With the high cost of living, many poor people today cannot buy the clothing their children need for school. In many areas thrift shops have been set up that sell second-hand clothing to the poor at a fraction of the cost.

This program is designed to collect second-hand clothing and channel it into the thrift shop nearest you. Many shops deal also in household items and furniture depending upon their facilities for storage. In most cases they have a very profitable business which proves the need for the operation.

Time Commitment

Flexible

Organization

- Contact your friends and ask them to inform you when they have old clothing they wish to donate.
- Contact your parish and see if a petition for old clothing can be included in your parish bulletin.
- Organize a clothing drive.
- Contact the chairmen of church organizations and have them make others aware that you are collecting old clothing.
- Find out when your "pet" thrift shop will receive clothing and inform those who have donations of their schedule.
- Arrange to have clothing picked up when the donor has no way to get the material to the shop.

Teenagers can often be asked to perform this pick-up service.

If You Wish to Begin Your Own Thrift Shop, you will need:

- Facilities. *A large room* for sales and *a smaller room* for receiving, sorting and pricing the materials; *tables* where clothing can be folded according to size and shape; *racks* where better clothing can be hung; large boxes about 45" cubed are sometimes used for similar items. This method of sorting is not as neat as the use of tables and racks, but can be an efficient method when space is at a premium.
- Pricing. Clothing can be priced according to the economic level of the people served. Some shops charge only $1.00 per shopping bag. Others charge about 1/10 the original cost of an item. Better articles are marked higher.
- Sales Persons. Frequently clubs or parish organizations will agree to staff the thrift shop one day a week. Usually at least two persons should be on duty at one time.
  NOTE: Request that all clothing be clean.

Resources

Guidelines for Neighborhood Community Organizing Community-Leader Training Association, Inc. 511 Monte Vista Drive, S.W. Blacksburg, Va. 24060
Some A B C's of Community Organization.

SEDFRE, Incorporated. 315 Seventh Avenue, Seventh Floor, New York, N.Y. 10001

Improving Participation in Voluntary Action. Center for A Voluntary Society. 1785 Massachusetts, N.W. Washington, D.C. 20036

Focus: Team Building. Center for a Voluntary Society. 1785 Massachusetts, N.W., Washington, D.C. 20036.

Meetings That Get Results. Community Leader Training Associates, Inc. 511 Monte Vista Drive, S.W. Blacksburg, Va. 24060.

PROTEINS FOR THE HUNGRY

We seldom think that people in America are hungry but there are three groups in our present society who have insufficient money to buy food. They are the elderly whose social security checks do not reach to the end of the month; those on welfare whose money cannot keep up with the rising cost of living, and the immigrants who have entered the country illegally. Even those who manage to eat regularly often have a nutritionally deficient diet.

"Proteins for the Poor" is a program designed to collect one can of high protein food from each family per month. This can be done as a parish or neighborhood project. The food is then channeled into one of the already existing food distribution centers in your area.

Time Commitment

Flexible. Two hours a week from each member of the organizing group should be sufficient to get the job done.

Organization

- Contact groups, parishes, clubs, etc. and ask them to enroll in the program and give one can of high protein food per month for distribution to the poor.
- Locate facilities that can serve as a food receiving center. Here food will be collected until delivered to the distribution center. It should be secure from theft.
- Choose a food distribution center where you can bring your collection regularly. Your welfare agency can give you the names of these centers.
- Ask teenagers to help in staffing the receiving center at certain hours. They can also be called upon to carry the food to the distribution center.
- Ask parishes of all denominations to designate one Sunday per month when people would be asked to bring their donation.

Orientation

Many people still think that no one needs to go hungry in our country. It is necessary to educate people on the very real problems that exist today for the elderly, the poor and others. Call upon someone involved in social action in your community to give you a talk on poverty in America, its causes and its widespread existence. Social Workers are usually qualified in this area.

Resources

Nutrition for the Elderly. Administration on Aging, Social and Rehabilitation Service, HEW. 330 Independence Avenue, S.W. Washington, D.C. 20201. (free)

Food and Housing for the Elderly. Food and Nutrition Service. U.S. Department of Agriculture, Washington, D.C. 20250 (free)

You Can Help Fight Hunger in America. Office of Communication Department of Agriculture, Washington, D.C. 20250 (free).

Issue Packet: Hunger and Development. The American Freedom from Hunger Foundation, 1717 H Street, N.W., Washington, D.C. 20250.

Hunger, U.S.A. Beacon Press, Order Department, Boston, Massachusetts. 02109

Publications List: Community Organizing to End Hunger. The Children's Foundation, 1028 Connecticut Avenue, N.W. Suite 614, Washington, D.C. 20036

Bread For the World. Arthur Simon. New York: Paulist Press, 1975.

NUTRITION EDUCATION

The poor and immigrant groups in this country often need a knowledge of how to prepare nutritious meals at a minimum cost. This program is designed to set up an educational program to provide this information. Its purpose is to give people the basic elements of good nutrition and food preparation.

Time Requirement for Organization

Depending upon your organizational ability and background, this program can be time-consuming.

Orientation

None needed.

Qualifications for Leadership

- experience in education at some level;
- organizational ability;
- knowledge of nutrition, or the ability to contact persons equipped to plan a profitable course;
- if you plan to work with the Spanish-speaking community, a knowledge of Spanish would be helpful.

How to Set Up the Program

- Gather a group of interested persons to help with the planning of the program.
- Survey the particular needs of your area. Do you need the program primarily for the poor, the black or the Spanish-speaking community?
- Check with parishes, schools, housing developments, senior citizen residences and community centers for an estimated participation.
- Find a convenient location to hold the course, a parish hall or community center that the prospective students can reach easily without a transportation problem.
- Look for teachers competent to teach nutrition, meal planning, consumer buying, etc. Try: 4-H Clubs, Extension Programs, YWCA, nurses and dieticians from hospitals and nursing homes.

Agencies That Can Help You

Welfare Agency

Office of the Aging
Board of Education
YWCA
YMCA
Council of Churches
Parish Councils
Jewish Federation

Resources

Food is More than Just Something to Eat. Food, Nutrition and Health Campaign, General Foods Corporation, 250 North Street, White Plains, New York. 10625 (free)

Consumer Food Economics, Department of Human Resources, Social Rehabilitation Administration, 122 C Street, N.W., Room 809 Washington, D.C. 20001 (free)

Food: A Key to Better Health. The Nutrition Foundation, Inc. 888 Seventeenth Street, N.W., Washington, D.C. 20006

You Can Help Fight Hunger in America. Office of Communication, Department of Agriculture, Washington, D.C. 20250 (free)

Donated Foods Handbook for Volunteers. (Same address as above-free)

Child Nutrition Programs Handbook for Volunteers. (Same address as above-free)

Food & Nutrition: Supplemental Lessons for Training Extension Aids. Superintendent of Documents, U.S. Government Printing Office, Washington, D.C. 20402.

Food Needs of Family Members. (Same address as above)

Meal Planning. (Same address as above)

Nutrition: Better Eating for a Head Start. Office of Child Development, U.S. Department of Health, Education & Welfare, Washington, D.C. 20201 (free)

Food Buying Guide & Recipes. (Same address as above—free)

A Guide of Food Stamps. American Friends Service Committee, 160 North Fifteenth Street, Philadelphia, Pa. 19102 (free)

CONSUMER EDUCATION

People in the inner-city and immigrant groups often need consumer education in order to make their small incomes reach to the end of the month. Many do not know how to work from a budget, how to buy food at the lowest cost, and particularly the way to buy medicine. If you live in or near a large city and know groups that need this service, the contribution you would make by beginning such a project would be great.

Time Commitment

This is a time-consuming project and needs a group of people who have some knowledge of educational programs.

Qualifications for the Leadership

● organizational ability,

- an understanding of the nature and possibilities of consumer education,
- contact with people who could be called upon as resources,
- good public relations.

How to Set up the Program

- Survey the particular needs of the community.
- Explore the sources of teachers for the program (colleges, extension programs, high schools).
- Explore the sources of potential students who would profit from the course.
- Choose facilities that are convenient for the projected student body. People needing this type of education have little transportation available to them.
- Decide on time, dates of the program.
- Estimate the cost of the program. It is suggested that you charge at least a minimum fee.
- Publicize the program in newspapers, parish bulletins, radio spots. Have posters in stores, senior residences, housing developments.

Resources

Fulfilling Consumer Rights, Chamber of Commerce of the United States Urban Strategy Center, 1615 H Street, N.W., Washington, D.C. 20006
S. & H. Consumer Services Guide, The Sperry & Hutchinson Co., Consumer Services, 2900 West Seminary Drive, Fort Worth, Texas. 76133 (free)

How to Be a Better Shopper. The Sperry & Hutchinson Co., Consumer Services, 2900 West Seminary Drive, Fort Worth, Texas 76133 (free)

Suggested Guidelines for Consumer Education. Superintendent of Documents, U.S. Government Printing Office, Washington, D.C. 20402 (Order # PR 3 68: 026/Ed 8)

Moving Ahead With Co-ops. Cooperative League of the USA. Suite 1100, 1828 L Street, N.W. Washington, D.C. 20036

OURS: How to Organize a Co-op. (Same address as above.)

Co-op Depot Manual (Same address as above)

Moving Ahead with Group Action: The Buying Club. (Same address as above.)

The Preparation & Organization of a Community Buying Club. Technical Resources Information Union, ACTION, Room M 1106, 806 Connecticut Avenue, N.W., Washington, D.C. 20525 (free)

The Booklet Can Help You Implement Your Program to Protect Consumers. New York State Consumer Protection Board, 270 Broadway, New York, N.Y. 10017 (free)

National Directors of Services for Low Income Consumer. Office of Economic Opportunity, Special Programs Division, Executive Office of the President, Washington, D.C. 20506 (free)

Coop Stores and Buying Clubs. (Same address as above—free)

Your Neighbor in Need—of a Credit Union. (Address same as above—free)

Food Stamp Sales Program for Limited Income Credit Union. (Same address as above—free)

INFORMATION AND REFERRAL

Within any given area are numerous community service agencies whose services are little known and under-utilized. This program is designed to provide information about the types of help that can be received from the various organizations.

Time Commitment

The organization of the program can consume a considerable amount of time. Once organized it will require a specific number of hours per week from each participant.

Orientation

Initially the program must prepare each person involved with a thorough knowledge of where to go in the community for various kinds of services. A good manual can do much to solve this problem, but a personal knowledge of each organization is essential.

- Have each member of your group visit agencies and report back on what they have learned.
- Have representatives from the various agencies speak to your group on their work.
- Have someone from FISH or Community Action speak on the Referral Services in the area.

How to Get the Program Off the Ground

- Get a current copy of community services in your area.
- Become familiar with each service and the contact people.

- Interest your friends in taking turns at being on call for people who need help.
- Set up a telephone network so that one person is assigned to take calls for each day of the week.

Resources

Organization & Operation of an Information, Referral and Follow-up Program. National Easter Seal Society, 2023 West Ogdon Avenue, Chicago, Illinois 60612

Handbook for Community Fact-Finders. American Friends Service Committee, 160 North 15th Street, Philadelphia, Pa. 19102

Question & Answer on the Information and Referral and Follow-up Program. National Easter Seal Society, 2023 West Ogdon Avenue, Chicago, Illinois 60612

Planning for a Telephone Ministry. Contact Teleministries USA. 900 So. Arlington Avenue, Room 125. Harrisburg, Pa. 17109 (free)

Basic Handbook. (Same address as above)

Focus on Active Listening and Referral. Housing Listening Post, State Office of Volunteer Programs, 701 Dayton, Edmonds, Washington, 98020 (free)

FUND RAISING

Many worthwhile projects flounder for lack of

funds. There is a vital need to raise money for most institutions, homes for children and charitable enterprises. Those who enjoy this challenging task can perform a valuable service in organizing programs for this purpose.

Time Commitment

It will depend on you but it can take a real commitment in time.

Orientation

Motivation of those who join you in the enterprise is essential. Some of the things you can do to stimulate interest and commitment on the part of the members are:

● Have a member of the organization or institution who will receive your funds give a talk on their work and activities.
● Ask other fund-raising groups to give you ideas on projects they found to be successful.
● Have someone speak who can create an awareness of the need for this kind of service.

Leadership Qualifications

● organizational ability,
● good public relations,
● creativity,
● dedication to a cause that needs money.

Getting the Program Started

● Gather a group of interested persons who will

help to organize a series of fund-raising events or
join a group already in existence.
● Choose a worthy cause that will inspire interest
and enthusiasm.
● Set up a schedule of events with a chairperson for
each event.
● Organize a public relations committee that will
utilize all forms of media to publicize events:
newspaper articles, radio spots, parish bulletins,
flyers in libraries and schools, telephone chains.

Programs that are good fund-raising ventures include:

● fashion shows,
● foreign or home travel tours,
● trips to your nearest race track,
● raffles,
● dinners,
● theatre parties,
● card parties.

Resources

*Manual of Practical Fund-Raising: Raising Funds
for Projects Serving Low-Income People.* VITA,
115 Gainsborough Street, Boston, Massachusetts
02115
Funding Kit. National Student Volunteer Program,
ACTION, 806 Connecticut Avenue, N.W., Washington, D.C. 20525 (free)
How to Build a Long-Term Fund Program. Motivation Inc., Stanford, Connecticut 06907

The Fund Development Handbook. Motivation Inc.,
   Stanford, Connecticut 06907
Ways and Means Handbook. The Sperry & Hutchinson Co., Consumer Services, 2900 West Seminary Drive, Fort Worth, Texas 76133

V
Citizen Participation in Government

Kevin Dunagan, S.J.
Sr. Diane Salt, SMIC

MAKING GOVERNMENT RESPONSIVE

There are a number of activities a concerned citizen may engage in to further the cause of justice. Most often that concern is translated into charitable efforts of social service. Action to relieve social injustices which have become institutionalized must also be the concern of citizens. Certain types of legislative action are designed to meet those problems that become systematized and require broad-based, continued effort.

The primary reason for government concern is to obtain justice by legislative action. Many individual and organizational actions put "band-aids" on social problems. What is needed is for equal energy to be applied to fixing up the machinery that produces the social problems. State legislatures are one large and specific part of that machinery. Many remedies, which are available in no other place, can be found

71

in activities that get laws passed or changed on a state level. Concern to influence the decisions that government makes, the laws that government passes, and the way government implements those laws and policies is an excellent means for furthering the cause of justice. Many factors are involved in reaching public political decisions. Citizens can and should be involved in any and all of the stages of this process, but are generally unfamiliar with it. To make matters worse, a vacuum exists between governments and the people, because citizens do not know who their representatives are or how they voted on issues. Responsive government can only result from the hard work of citizens, and it is in their best interest and the best interest of peoples who are oppressed to take on some of this hard work.

What is the incentive for involvement in legislative action? Why should individuals or groups take on the task of monitoring legislation and calling into account the state government?

Gains—Purposes

The concern here is with *action* on issues and accountability of government. Such activity has these purposes:

1. To *emphasize* the impact the ordinary citizen has on legislation. Never underestimate your power or your ability to influence government. Elected officials are in positions of power, but people are power because they represent votes; votes for legislators' election or re-election; votes supporting legislators' key bills. Just as the American economy belongs to the people, so too does the legislature.

2. To *explain* the method for strategizing to encourage the passage of certain bills. Invaluable knowledge of the workings of government is gained by direct involvement in the workings.

3. To *educate* regarding social justice topics. Action on legislation advances social justice for many sectors of the population, and provides an opportunity, not only to be informed but to exert influence where change can be effective.

The Fundamental How?

How do we go about it? There are basic points to keep in mind when organizing citizens' groups to be concerned about affecting state legislation.

1. *Determine Goals—Resources.* Your group must establish a system suitable to its resources and needs. You should establish a means for dealing with state government after goal setting and evaluation of your capabilities. ACTION IS THE KEY—NOT MEETINGS. ESTABLISH A SYSTEM OF CONTACT. GET PEOPLE TO WRITE. ATTEND "HOW-TO" WORKSHOPS.

The big question to ask here is "Do we want to be an information gathering group, or an action organization?" For this you need to know the greatest need in your area. In other words, are people basically well informed and ready to act, but lack access to state assembly? Or, are people less ready to act because they are more in need of education? The answers to these questions will determine the type of mechanism you set up to begin to respond to the needs of your area and your state legislature.

You may not be ready for action. You may want to concentrate on the *workings* of the state legisla-

ture and on how a bill becomes a law. You may need
to spend time with *local officials* and other concerned
groups to determine what issue you want to work on.
Here again, you may rely on the resources of such
established groups as the League of Women Voters
and Common Cause and you may wish to secure
publications from your state department or films
from your local library to describe the legislative
process of your state.

You may need a series of *educational* meetings to
lay the ground work for action. Another option edu-
cationally may be for your group to present its program to local candidates before *elections*. Such activity is initiative, not reactionary and may go a long
way toward influencing legislators throughout the
year.

Your group may decide that a simple *telephone
network* to act on legislation is the best avenue to
follow. This is a simple enough thing to set up and
requires only that someone know the concerns of the
group and know when action is being taken on legislation regarding that issue.

Another option is a *letter-writing campaign*. Letters do have an impact on legislators. A significant
number of letters has a significant impact. Many letters can turn a legislator's attention and may even
change his mind. It is safe to say that a few thousand
letters significantly influence the work of a state legislature on any given issue.

You could begin an action such as designing and
disseminating a small newsletter describing the
whole legislative process and continuing presentation
of issues.

Know your capabilities. You may want to and

have the expertise to initiate legislation. On the other hand, your members may not have the time for the issue research necessary for writing legislation, so you would have to confine your efforts to support measures.

2. *Connectability.* Remember to tie in with other groups. You can devise a simple program for your group and may wish to tie this into larger organizations, such as Common Cause or the League of Women Voters, which have state and county chapters, or the Office of Government Concern of the State Council of Churches. All of these groups may provide support as well as research and action ideas for your group. You, in turn, can assist them by being the votes and the voices for their causes.

Where to start is always a crucial question. If you are a member of a parish group, you may wish to start there. Also, School PTA's, local civic groups, or special interest groups, such as Friends of Welfare. All of these people have a concern, or should have a concern, about what is happening on a state level in terms of legislation because all are affected in one way or another by the decisions on school budgets, community service programs, housing, and most state laws.

3. *Select Issues.* Here three basic principles should be kept in mind.

a. For your action to succeed, it must appeal to some level of self-interest of the people with whom you're working. The issue of state fluoridation of the water system may not be a concern to your group. However, laws regarding the drafting of a new school tax system, based on property value, may be a concern especially if it means raising your taxes a fair amount.

b. Your issues should be broad to include others outside your own group and to speak to the broader injustices other than those affecting your own environment. This goes back to the point about tying in with other groups. You may have to translate your concern for a stop sign at the corner of a particular street into the broader issue of public safety in order to get the support of the other groups.

c. Be careful to choose issues you have time and expertise to research, especially if you are not relying on the resources of the other groups. For example, penal reform is a very broad issue. If no other groups are researching it or can act as a resource, you may have a hard time doing your own research with limited volunteer personnel and limited funds.

4. *The Public Should Know.* Publicity is an important thing to keep in mind. If you do have a speaker come to your group or hold a public meeting with candidates, or if a significant number of your members take action on an issue, you should do so publicly. Besides writing letters and making phone calls, an occasional release to a newspaper will put your action in the public forum, and will suggest to other concerned citizens ways they can lend their support. It will, of course, be a reminder to other members of the state legislature.

When You Write

Now let us say a word about the tools that can be

used in any campaign or system designed to effect legislation on the state level. First of all, writing is one of the principal tools. Letters do carry weight with legislators and many have been known to say that as few as 25 letters will make them take serious notice. Keep in mind that responses must be quick and effective, and therefore not the least bit vague. A good personal letter from a voter in the election district is one of the most effective means of influencing legislators' positions on pending legislation. Remember the following points in writing your letter:

1. Be sure you know who your state legislators are. Know in which legislative district you are. Identify your state senator and assemblyman who represent you.

2. Know your state legislators' full name. Use this and the preferred mailing address in writing.

3. Use your full name and address. Make sure they are both legible. Identify yourself as a registered voter in his/her district.

4. Use the proper form of address and salutation both in letters and on envelopes. For state senators, the Honorable _____. For Assemblymen, the Honorable_____.

5. Identify the bill in which you are interested. Lawmakers usually remember them by number, and a short nickname. Check carefully to be sure you are talking about the right bill.

6. Give reasons for the position you take. Your own personal experience is your best supporting evidence. Be specific. Let the legislators

know how this measure affects their own election district.

7. Time your letter. Mail should arrive while a bill is being readied for consideration and needs your support. When the bill is before them, the state legislators are able to relate your ideas to the proposal.

8. Follow the bill's progress for good timing; when to send your letters can be determined if you maintain a continuous interest in legislative issues. Follow the progress of bills with your group or by contacting your local legislative representative.

9. Short letters are most effective. Don't be wordy. Limit your letter to one subject. One typed page is usually sufficient. Express yourself pleasantly and effectively. Threats, scolding, intimidation, or insincere flattery will not win their help or cooperation.

10. A reply is not necessary if you suspect your state legislator is receiving many letters on this issue. Indicate that politely in your letter.

11. Don't use form letters, printed postcards, or copy another person's letter. Let legislators know this is your own personal opinion. Use plain or personal stationery.

12. Do not ask sponsors to vote for their own bills. The legislator's name on the bill as a sponsor is a commitment to a yes vote. Thank sponsors instead, and ask them to get the bill up for a floor vote.

Permanent Newsletter—Network

Now let's talk about a more permanent contact

tool. As has been said, letter writing, telephone networks, public meetings, and pre-election campaigns are all means of dealing with and calling into account your state legislative system. Your group may be ready and interested in a more permanent tool to keep this process of citizen involvement moving. One model might be an action-response newsletter. Such a letter would be issued periodically, and would contain:

1. The issue and explanation of the bill.
2. The position of the group on the bill. Select a position. Ask the writer if he agrees. Don't leave room for choice.
3. The situation of the bill (that is, the problems regarding the legislation and where it is in the legislative process).
4. The need for action (pinpoint the action needed to remedy the situation, that is, if the bill is bogged down in committee what legislators are on that committee who are holding it up? Who needs to be contacted?).
5. Whom to write to (names and addresses of who should be contacted regarding action to be taken).

If your group is large enough, and if you are linked with other groups you may even want to charge a minimal fee for this service. This tells people this service is necessary and important. It also calls for a commitment for the subscriber to act. And finally, it pays for your expenses.

Success

If your group moves in this direction, remember that your group will need to feel its influence. It will need to know it has been effective. Therefore, it is important to keep some form of scorecard which will let your members know what action was taken on bills that you supported or didn't support, and how many times your influence was felt.

Resources

Let us say a word about resources before our final comment on how a bill becomes law. There are, of course, a number of important resources that can be a help in this venture. Some of them have been mentioned already.

Organizations

1. *Common Cause,* a citizens' lobby group with state and county chapters.
2. *League of Women Voters*, a national organization with state chapters which monitor state legislation and support legislation in favor of human development.
3. Council of Churches, Office of Government Concern.
4. State Catholic Conference.

Publications

- *Publications* of state legislature.
- *Minutes* of committee meetings—most state legislatures publish the proceedings of all hearings and committee meetings.
- *The Legislative Index*—This is published by your state legislature. It includes a list of all bills that

have been filed by category, and the status of the bill. In other words, citizens can find at a glance all bills that have been introduced regarding public transportation. The bills will be listed by number with the names of the sponsors and will indicate the number of hearings the bill has been given and what committee the bill is now in.

- *The Legislative Manual*—This is available in most libraries and most schools and describes your state legislative system.
- *Copies of Bills*—These are generally available from your state house office of bills or may be obtained from any legislators who are sponsors of the bill.

Other

- Legislative *hotlines*—Many states issue a toll free number that citizens can call to determine the status of a bill, when committees are meeting, and what bills are currently under consideration at any given time.

STATE LEGISLATIVE SYSTEM

Now a word about how the state legislatures are set up and the process of how a bill becomes a law. It must be obvious by now that it is important for all concerned citizens' groups to understand the physical set up of their legislature and the process by which a bill becomes a law. Citizen input at all points of this process has much to do with the final result. Knowledge of the process of a bill in the state legislature facilitates the ability of a group to respond.

State legislatures differ in a number of aspects, but there are certain characteristics that are common to most. These include:

1. Bicameral—The Senate plus General Assembly.
2. One house, usually the Senate, must approve most of the Governor's nominations for state executive and judicial positions. The other house, usually the General Assembly, must originate new programs for raising revenue.
3. A Constitutional amendment must originate in the legislature and be approved by voters in a general election. Proposed Constitutional amendments, therefore, go directly from the legislature to the people.
4. To finance capital expenditures over and above the approved percent (usually 1% of the annual appropriations) the legislature must propose a bond issue. This must be approved in a general election.
5. Each branch of the legislature elects leadership, establishes rules and committees, and makes committee assignments. The senate leader is the President. The Assembly leader is the Speaker of the Assembly.
6. Sessions of each house vary. In some states, legislators serve full time. In most states, this is not true. Members are generally in session two days a week for about 6 months of the year.
7. Committee meetings and party conferences are a big part of the legislator's day. This is important to remember, because some citizen efforts

should perhaps be generated in having these meetings open so that citizens input can be felt.

The following is an outline of the stages of the legislative process on the state level for New Jersey:

HOW A BILL BECOMES LAW
(League of Women Voters of New Jersey)

1. Bill is examined for wording, statement of purpose, fiscal note.

2. The clerk of the Assembly or secretary of the Senate gives the bill 1st reading.[1] The presiding officer assigns the bill to committee or advances the bill with no reference directly to 2nd reading.

3. The committee may take no action, report unfavorably, report favorably with no changes, amend, report a committee substitute, hold a public hearing.[2]

4. If a bill is reported out of committee or sent without reference it receives automatic 2nd reading. Amendments may be offered only when a bill is at 2nd reading.

5. The presiding officer prepares the calendar (list) of bills to be considered at 3rd reading.[3] Bills are debated from the floor at this time. If the bill is to be amended it must move back to 2nd reading. After passage the bill moves to the second house or to the Governor.[4]

6. To amend a bill at the time of floor debate an emergency resolution is required to move the bill from 3rd reading back to 2nd reading. If final action is desired on the same day another emergency reso-

lution is required to advance the bill, amended or not, back to 3rd reading.

7. Upon delivery to the second house the bill must proceed along the same path of 1st, 2nd and 3rd reading. If the bill is amended in the second house either in committee or on the floor it must return to the house of origin for concurrence with amendments.

8. The Governor has 10 days in which to sign the bill or veto it.[5] If vetoed, the bill returns to the Legislature. If he takes no action within 10 days the bill becomes law.[6]

9. The Legislature can let the veto stand; can override it by 2/3 vote in each house; or by a majority in each house the Legislature can concur with the amendments recommended by the Governor and send the bill back for his signature.

Legislative Terms

Bill—a proposed statute or law. Each bill is assigned a number and prefixed with an A or S depending on its house of origin. Bills are referred to as S.*000* (Senate Bill 000) A.*0000* (Assembly Bill 0000). Must pass both houses and be signed by the Governor.

Resolution—a formal resolution by one house expressing the policy or opinion of the house adopting it. It is designated and referred to as AR 00 (Assembly Resolution 00) or SR 00 (Senate Resolution 00). Needs approval only of the house which proposes it.

Joint Resolution—a formal resolution separately adopted by both houses, requires the approval of the

Governor. Has the effect of law and is used in lieu of a bill when enactment is temporary, or for the purpose of initiating a study or to recommend something to the U.S. Congress (called "memorializing"). Referred to as AJR 00 or SJR 00.

Concurrent Resolution—a resolution adopted by both houses expressing the will of the Legislature. Can be used for memorials, commendation, legislative organizational matters or to set up study commissions not involving gubernatorial appointments. Its effect expires at the end of the two-year term of the Legislature adopting it. It is also the procedure used to propose constitutional amendments. Referred to as ACR 00 or SCR 00.

Procedure

Many procedures are established by rules adopted by each house at the beginning of each two-year term and therefore are subject to change.

The chart (reverse side) shows procedures for passing a typical bill. After a bill is introduced it is referred to an appropriate committee. Recent rules require votes taken in committee be made in open session. There are also requirements for advance notice of committee meetings, including agendas. Committee reports on attendance and voting records are public records.

By tradition no bill is acted upon unless the sponsor requests it, nor can it be moved on the floor of the house by anyone but the sponsor. A bill that has passed one house is usually moved in the second house by a legislator from the same district or county as the prime sponsor.

Fiscal notes usually accompany bills involving expenditure of state revenues. These are prepared by the Office of Fiscal Affairs. Both houses now require review by the Appropriations Committees of bills requiring expenditures more than $100,000.

Debate in both houses is limited to the bill under consideration. In the General Assembly members may speak three times on each bill—15 minutes the first two times, 5 minutes the third.

Senators may also speak three times on each bill —30 minutes the first time, 15 the second, and 5 the third.

Both houses have electronic voting boards mounted on the walls. The number of the measure under consideration is posted and the members' votes are recorded and automatically tabulated. The member casts his Aye (green light) or Nay (red light) by operating a switch from his desk. Both houses require the presence of the legislator on the floor for his vote to be recorded. Both houses may be placed "under call" which action prohibits legislators from leaving the floor. Any legislator recorded as present when the house is "under call" will have his vote registered as negative to the measure if he abstains or leaves his desk.

Nominations by the Governor requiring Senate approval are referred to the Senate Judiciary Committee. Tradition, referred to as senatorial courtesy, gives any senator from the home county of a nominee veto power over the nomination. Approval of the appointment of current or former legislators to a state post is usually automatic.

The Constitution requires a public hearing be held on a proposed constitutional amendment 20 days before it may be considered in the house of origin. Should it be amended, another hearing must be held twenty days before it can come up for a vote.

There is no requirement for public hearings on bond issues which go on the ballot. Legislative committees sometimes hold public hearings on the more important measures they consider.

THE VOTES IT TAKES TO . . . .

. . . *pass a bill*, a majority vote of 41 in the Assembly, 21 in the Senate.

. . . *amend a bill on the floor*, a majority of those present and voting.

. . . *demand a roll call vote*, 16 in the Assembly, 8 in the Senate (1/5).

. . . *put a constitutional amendment on the ballot*, 48 in the Assembly, 24 in the Senate (3/5), or an amendment can go on the ballot if it passes both houses by a *majority* in two successive legislative years.

. . . *override a veto by the Governor*, 54 in the Assembly, 27 in the Senate (2/3).

. . . *approve a nomination*, 21 in the Senate.

. . . *move a bill on emergency procedures*, 60 in the Assembly, 30 in the Senate (3/4).

. . . *adopt a motion on the floor*, a majority of those present and voting, in most cases. Motions to reconsider a bill or any action taken must get the same number of votes as required to pass the bill or take the action in the first place.

FOOTNOTES

1. A bill is "read" by number and title only. Bills are never read in their entirety at any time during the three obligatory readings.
2. A majority vote of the committee members is required to report out a bill. In the Assembly, if a sponsor has requested

committee action three times and the committee has not taken a vote for or against the bill, the Conference Committee may direct the committee to report the bill on a vote representing 41 assemblymen. In the Senate, the presiding officer can move a bill from its committee to the Conference & Coordinating Committee. In the Senate a committee can be relieved of a bill 60 days after the sponsor submits a written request. In both houses, a sponsor can, upon twenty-four hours notice and with the signature of a majority of the members of his house on a discharge petition, get a bill out of committee. To hold a public hearing requires a majority vote of committee members.

3. Under the Constitution one calendar day must elapse between 2nd and 3rd reading. This may be waived under an emergency resolution.

4. On 3rd reading bills that are not passed may be (1) *laid on the table* if a motion is adopted prior to the announcement of roll call; (2) *reconsidered* upon request of one who voted on the prevailing side, with concurrence of the majority to proceed, and providing the bill originally received 15 votes in the Senate, 30 in the Assembly; (3) *recommitted* upon motion by the sponsor and a majority vote; (4) *defeated*.

5. The Governor may conditionally veto a bill, sending it back to the Legislature with recommendations for amendments; he may veto line items in an appropriations bill without vetoing the entire bill.

6. The Governor has 45 days (excluding Sundays) to act on those bills delivered to him *within 10 days of the end of the two-year legislative term*. He may sign the bill into law, veto it, or "pocket-veto" it by not signing. Thus, at the end of a legislative term the Governor can kill a bill by not signing it as well as by vetoing it.

VI
Fact and Action Ideas on World Hunger

Sr. Diane Salt, SMIC

"We Christians . . . are ourselves responsible for the misuse of the resources God has given to the world. And our responsibility is not merely as person for other people, but also for the political and economic structures that bring about poverty, injustice and violence. Today our responsibility has a new dimension because men would now have the power to remove the causes of the evil, whose symptoms alone they could treat before."

> *Report of the Beirut Conference on World Development sponsored by the World Council of Churches and the Pontifical Commission on Justice and Peace, 1968.*

Over the past decade, men throughout the world have grown in awareness of the terrible inequality in

the distribution of resources among nations. The fact
that countries like our own can spend millions of
dollars on advertising high-protein dog food while
countless people die from starvation stings our con-
sciences. We are slowly growing in the realization
that man must work toward new structures that will
promote a just sharing of those materials needed for
the perservation of life; yet, in our complex society,
we often feel helpless in deciding what steps will effect a remedy.

Hunger has been with us since the origins of man
and, it will not disappear overnight. Yet, there are
actions that each man can take to facilitate the process of eliminating this basic evil. Here are a few
ideas:

1.	**FACT:**	In the United States, as much as one-third of the dog and cat food sold in city slums is being eaten by people. *Times Union* June 20, 1974
	ACTION:	Collect food for one of your Food Distribution Centers. Have families donate one can of high-protein food per month to this cause.
2.	**FACT:**	There are 1 ½ billion people who are continually hungry in Africa, India, Southeast Asia, Latin America, Bangladesh, United States.
	FACT:	The same amount of food that is feeding 210 million Americans would feed 1.5 billion Chinese on an average Chinese diet.

FACT: A saving of about 100 calories a day or around 3% of the food that Americans buy would be equivalent to what is needed to provide a supplemental and probably life-saving diet of 1,000 calories a day to 21 million people in the less-developed countries.

ACTION: Lower consumption. Don't waste food. This does not imply a less-nourishing diet, but merely an increased consciousness of food value and the determination to eat simple but nutritional meals.

ACTION: Eat one meatless meal a week and contribute your savings to any of the special relief projects founded for the hunger emergency:

American Freedom From Hunger Foundation
1100 17th Street, N.W.
Washington, D.C. 20036

Bread for the World
602 E 9th Street
New York, N.Y.

Catholic Relief Services
350 Fifth Avenue
New York, N.Y. 10001

CROP
Box 214
Rocky Hill, New Jersey 08553

3. FACT: 80% of multi-national investments

in developing countries has no bearing on such essential needs as food production;

ACTION: Secure information from the Interfaith Center for Corporate Responsibility, Room 566, 475 Riverside, New York, N.Y. 10027

View with your interest group the ABC news close-up: "Food-Green Grow the Profits" Available from:
MacMillan Films, Inc.
34 MacQuesten Parkway South
Mount Vernon, N.Y. 10550
Attn: Mrs. Dorothy Dunbar
(914) 664-5051

4. **FACT:** It is estimated that in Latin America 1,000,000 children are at present in a severe state of malnutrition and 10,000,000 are suffering from moderate malnutrition. In Africa, about 3,000,000 children are affected by severe malnutrition and 16,000,000 by moderate malnutrition. In Asia, the corresponding figures are 6,000,000 and 64,000,000.

FACT: Taking the world as a whole, about 10,000,000 children are at great risk of death, and even if treated, one-third of them would probably still die from hunger and malnutrition. In addition, the condition of 90,000,000 children with moderate forms of malnutrition may suddenly be aggravated by infection.

ACTION: Have a missionary speak to your club, school, Parish Council on the problem of hunger.

5. FACT: Voices of caring persons are being raised around the world. From the Gospel itself, through almost 2000 years of history, the Church has seen the social apostolate as much a part of its essential mission as the proclamation of the Word and the celebration of the sacraments.

This current focus on the problem of hunger—very tangible, fairly comprehensible even to the well fed —may be offering us, as a Church, one of our finest opportunities to renew within ourselves an awareness of our human brotherhood, interdependence and community.

ACTION: Develop with the assistance of the Social Action Committee and/or the Mission Society and/or the school Human Rights Club a method for regularly collecting parish contributions saved through eating simple or meatless meals.

ACTION: Take as a parish project the sharing of meatless recipes. Make a booklet of these recipes as a fund raiser for Catholic Relief Services or just for fun.

6. FACT: Almost all working roles provide
                clear opportunities to raise the con-
                sciences of others. Teachers have a
                special role to play. Classes on
                home economics, science, socio-
                political studies, geography, and lit-
                erature can be adapted to an under-
                standing of hunger, its effects, and
                the cultures and people of the third
                world. Religious leaders and teach-
                ers can explore the reactions of the
                scriptures to questions of hunger.
                Nutritionists, suppliers, farmers,
                restaurant owners, doctors, nurses,
                media people, union members,
                housewives, all these have much to
                contribute in their work. Careful
                study, planning and discussion can
                make a real difference.

    ACTION: Send for the report on the Panel on
                Nutrition and the International Sit-
                uation reporting to the Senate Se-
                lect Committee on Nutrition and
                Human Needs from the Govern-
                ment Printing Office, your Con-
                gressperson or the Senate Select
                Committee Office. The report notes
                several conditions in the U.S. that
                must be dealt with in order to meet
                the nation-wide and world-wide
                food needs.

7. FACT: Trade is an exchange freely agreed
                upon so that each secures a benefit.

That idea remains the working model of nations, but in practice the benefits tend to favor rich nations and to tag poor ones as losers.

FACT:　Protective tariffs and import quotas work a particular hardship on poor countries, which need to develop markets as they industrialize.

FACT:　Tariffs and quotas on goods result in higher prices, along with inflationary effects of those prices—a cost to the United States Consumer.

ACTION:　Along with the cut in the use of meat and fertilizer, public pressure must be brought to bear on the legislation protecting high profits, tariffs, and embargoes. Intensive lobbying by big business interests seeking subsidies and restrictions must be contrasted by citizens with humanitarian convictions.

ACTION:　Support low-interest, government loans for businesses and the farm sectors which suffer because of foreign imports so they can be competitive or can move into other areas of production.

8. FACT:　The dimensions of the world hunger situation are too vast to be solved merely by providing emergency food on a year-to-year, crisis-to-

crisis basis to maintain subsistence. National and international agencies, created to deal with the problem on a short-term basis, are neither sufficient or efficient.

ACTION: Americans must begin to attack on world hunger by recognizing the staggering dimensions of the problem, which involves not only immediate aid, but trade relations, environment development, land reform. Educate others in your Church and Community organizations to the necessity of providing a voice for developing nations into the consciousness of U.S. Policymakers.

9. **FACT:** Starvation and severe malnutrition are already the lot of millions of people throughout the world. An estimated 10,000 deaths a day are attributed directly to the lack of either enough food to sustain life or the right food to ward off disease.

FACT: This crisis is not a temporary phenomenon, part of the cyclical operation of the laws of the weather and of supply and demand, but an indication that food scarcity is becoming chronic.

ACTION: Urge the United States President, Secretary of the Interior and Secretary of State to have the U.S. lead in setting up the needed global reserve system and the mechanisms for poor countries to finance agriculture imports.

10. FACT: In fourteen hours, the Department of Defense outspends the entire budget of the United Nations Food and Agriculture Program.

ACTION: Urge your Congresspeople to:
Refocus United States aid (currently only .25 of 1% of the G.N.P.) on food, agricultural technology, and land reform rather than military aid.

11. FACT: A 70% increase in the price of oil, essential to the manufacturers of nitrate fertilizers, has caused a scarcity of fertilizer and higher prices. The U.S. therefore, put an embargo on the export of fertilizers to foreign countries, causing severe production problems for poorer countries.

FACT: If we were to export just the amount of fertilizer used in cemeteries and golf courses, we could ensure crop production in poorer countries.

ACTION: Refuse to use fertilizers for non-food producing use. For example, lawns, and flower gardens. Non-food use of fertilizer in the U.S. consumes 3,000,000,000 tons yearly.

12. FACT: The average American consumes
                   2,000 pounds of grain yearly. The
                   average Colombian or Chinese eats
                   400 pounds of grain yearly. Only
                   140 pounds of the American intake
                   is eaten directly as grain in bread
                   and cereal products. Of the Chinese
                   and Colombians' 400 pounds, 360 is
                   eaten directly.

    FACT: In 1973 the average American ate
                   119 pounds of meat yearly. High
                   meat consumption wastes valuable
                   grain and is not the most nutritional
                   way to provide protein. It takes five
                   pounds of grain to produce one
                   pound of meat. Grain fed to cattle
                   comes to the consumer with only
                   5% of the calories and protein of the
                   original grain.

    ACTION: Protein does not have to be supplied
                   by meat. Eat less meat. Substitute
                   chicken for beef. Chicken is about
                   three times more efficient than beef
                   in generating animal protein.

                   If Americans were to substitute
                   chicken for one-third of their beef
                   consumption, we would save enough
                   grain   to   adequately   feed
                   1,000,000,000 people every year. By
                   eating one less hamburger a week,
                   the equivalent grain saved would

feed a subsistence diet to 50,000,000 people.

13. FACT: The United States ranks fifteenth of seventeen among aid-giving nations on a per capita basis.

    FACT: Aid provided by the Marshall Plan of 1950 was 75% higher than the amount (2/10 of 1% of the G.N.P.) we now give.

    FACT: On January 23, 1974 the House of Representatives rejected a 1.5 million dollar loan to the International Development Agency.

    ACTION: Urge your Congresspeople to:
             A. Increase U.S. development aid to at least the United Nations standard of 7/10 of 1% of the Gross National Product.
             B. Bring Food for Peace assistance at least back to the 1972 level and eliminate the use of these revenues for arms.

14. FACT: A one-year intensive promotion will not solve the problem of world hunger. Money alone cannot solve this problem. This crisis is a call to a new awareness, personal, professional and social. The response to the needs of the hungry today calls for a careful long-range look at the way we live.

ACTION: Get the family involved, especially the kids with . . . *Creative Food Experiences for Children*—This book is a gold mine of activities, games, facts, and recipes that convey a sense of food as both interesting and fun. It is intended as a resource book for all adults who care about what children are eating and want to get children enthusiastic and involved in the production and preparation of food for themselves and others. It is ideal for school teachers, parents, nutritionists, and scout leaders. Available from:

Center for Science in the Public Interest
1779 Church Street N.W.
Washington, D.C. 20036

15. FACT: As demand for resources grows it becomes more and more urgent to conserve those that are left and to avoid those practices which can actually destroy a resource. Military practices, including war and the preparation for war consumes large amounts of natural resources. Often military consumption of scarce and non-renewable raw materials is on a priority basis. (Arthur H. Westing, "Arms Control and the Environment", *Science and Public Affairs*, January 1974, p. 24).

FACT: The conduct of modern war is becoming increasingly destructive of land, air, and water resources. "Military preparations have involved frequent accidents polluting the environment through nuclear weapons tests, the loss of nuclear bombs and leakage of toxic elements" (E.K. Fedorov, "The Interaction of Man and the Environment," *Science and Public Affairs*, February, 1972, p. 8). Chemical warfare, involved in such activities as rainmaking and the use of herbicides and defoliants, results in often unpredictable long-term damage.

ACTION: *Bread for the World*, A Christian citizens' movement attempting to engage the attention of political leaders to create U.S. policy addressing itself to the crisis of world hunger. Join with this responsible effort to effect the crucial political attitudes that will promote a stance of justice and concern to the poorest members of our global family.

16. FACT: Developed nations have a life style that demands large supplies of natural resources. Furthermore, they have large business conglomerates that have developed technology and that have capital available for in-

vestment and research. These large corporations often exercise great political and economic power, so that when developing nations ask for assistance, these large business concerns have a great deal of influence over what assistance will be given.

FACT: Rather than invest revenue in research to develop and adapt technology to the developing world, multinational corporations often arrange to sell existing technology in its present form. This is profitable for the corporation and is efficient in establishing factories in developing countries.

ACTION: Global Awareness Program: Introduce the concepts of global interdependence into the regular school curriculum. Resources are available, including those listed below:
> Global Associates
> 522 Park Avenue East
> Orange, N.J.

Resources

Bread For The World, Arthur Simon, Paulist Press.
Recipes For A Small Planet, Ellen Buchman Ewald, Ballantine Books

Diet For A Small Planet, Francis Moore Lappe, Ballantine Books

The Politics Of World Hunger, Paul and Arthur Simon, Harper books

Why Is The Third World Poor? Piero Gheddo, Orbis Books

The Contrasumers: A Citizen's Guide To Resource Conservation, Praeger books, 1974

Man And His Environment: Food by Lester Brown and Gail W. Finsterbusch, Harper and Row, 1972

Eater's Digest, The Consumer's Factbook of Food Additives, Michael F. Jacobson

Global Living Here and Now, James A. Scherer, Friendship Press, 1974

Impact/Hunger, Special Report of National Impact, 110 Maryland Avenue, N.E. Washington, D.C. 20002. Available in bulk

Starvation or Plenty, Colin Clark—Taplinger Publishing Company

The Geography of Hunger, Josue de Castro, Little

Attack on Starvation, Norman Derosier-Avi Publishing Company

By Bread Alone, Lester Brown and Eric Eckholm, Praeger

In The Human Interest, Lester Brown, Norton and Company

Old Recipes with New Ideas from the Clinical Research Center, College of Medicine, University of Iowa, Iowa City, Iowa 52250

When You Write to Washington. League of Women Voters of the U.S. 1730 M. Street, N.W. Washington, D.C. 20036

A Letterwriter's Guide to Congress. Chamber of Commerce of the U.S. 1615 H Street, N.W. Washington, D.C. 20006

Meeting with Your Congressman: How To Do and Questions to Ask. 1615 H. Street, N.W., Washington, D.C. 20006 (free)

Voluntary Association & Public Policy. The Journal. Todd Hill Road. Lakeside, Conn. 06758

Network. National Urban Coalition. 2100 M. Street, N.W., Washington, D.C. 20037 (free)

Search. The Urban Institute. 2100 M. Street, N.W. Washington, D.C. 20037 (free)

VII
Resources:
Books, Films, Plays, Slides

For Older Persons

Friends in Neighborly Service, Volunteer Action Center, 955 S.W. Second Avenue, Miami, Florida. 33130

A Guide for Friendly Visitors. State Department of Social Service, 1450 Western Avenue, Albany, New York. 12203 (free)

It's Good to Have/Be a Friend, Age Center of Worcester Area, Inc. 5 Main Street, Worcester, Massachusetts. 01608

The Older Volunteer in Mental Health. Community Service Society, 105 East 22nd Street, New York, New York. 10010 (free)

Guidelines for an Information & Counseling Service for Older Persons. Older Americans Resources & Service Program, Box 2914 Duke University Medical Center, Durham, North Carolina 27710

How to Publish a Telephone Directory for Older Persons. National Council of Jewish Women. 1 West 47th Street, New York, New York 10036

How to Organize a Senior Center. National Institute of Senior Citizens, 1828 L Street, N.W., Washington, D.C. 20036

Oregon's Booklet, Being a Trained Volunteer in

Nursing Homes and Homes for the Aged. Oregon State Health Division, Epidemiology Division, Tuberculosis and Chronic Diseases Unit, P.O. Box 231, Portland, Oregon 97207 (free)

Manual on Volunteer Services in Homes for the Aging & Nursing Homes. Texas Association of Homes for the Aging. P.O. Box 4553, Austin, Texas 78765

Volunteer Service Corps Handbook. American Nursing Home Association, 1025 Connecticut Avenue, N.W. Washington, D.C. 20036

Recreation in Nursing Homes, National Recreation & Park Association, 1601 North Kent Street, Arlington, Virginia 22209

Dance Therapy Program for Nursing Homes (Hand Dances) Unitarian Universalist Women's Federation, 25 Beacon Street, Boston, Massachusetts 02108

Your Retirement Hobby Guide. AARP/NRTA, 1909 K Street, N.W., Washington, D.C. 20006 (free)

After 65: Resources for Self-Reliance. Public Affairs Pamphlets, 381 Park Avenue South, New York, New York. 10016

Films

"I Think They Call Him John". Mass Media Ministries, 1720 Chouteau Avenue, St. Louis, Missouri. 63103

"The Stringbean". Mass Media Ministries (Same address as above)

"The Yellow Leaf". Kent State University Audiovisual Services, Kent, Ohio 44242.

On Crime Prevention

Volunteers Help Youth. National Center for Voluntary Action. Clearinghouse, 1785 Massachusetts Avenue, N.W. Washington, D.C. 20036 (free)

Boys' Clubs & Delinquency Prevention. Boys' Clubs of America, 771 First Avenue, New York, N.Y. 10017. (free)

Listeners. Broward County Division of Youth Services. 303 S.E. Seventeenth Street, Suite 302, Fort Lauderdale, Florida. 33316.

Neighborhood Service Centers. Superintendent of Documents, U.S. Government Printing Office, Washington, D.C. 20402. (Order # GPO 1760-0011 FS14)

Delinquency Prevention Through Youth Development. Office of Youth—Office of Human Development, Department of Health, Education and Welfare, Washington, D.C. 20201. (free)

Are You the Key Person We are Looking For? Marocopa County Juvenile Court Center, 3125 West Durango, Phoenix, Arizona. 85009 (free)

Films

"Criminal Justice in the United States" University of Minnesota, Audio Visual Department.

"The Odds Against". University of Minnesota, Audio Visual Department.

"Until I Die". Video Nursing. P.O. Box 192, Evanston, Illinois 60204

On Transportation Programs

SOS-4 *Developing Transportation Services for the Older Person.* National Council on the Aging, 1828 L Street, N.W. Washington, D.C. 20036

Publications & Films on Aging, Institute on Gerontology, The University of Michigan, 543 Church Street, Ann Arbor, Michigan 48104 (free)

Volunteer Drivers, National Center for Voluntary Action, 1785 Massachusetts Avenue, N.W., Washington, D.C. 20036. (free)

Education

How to Treat the Adult Illiterate. National Affiliation for Literacy Advance, Laubach Literacy, Inc. P.O. Box 131, Syracuse, N.Y. 13210

Volunteer: Handbook for Adult Education Volunteers. Huntsville Area Vocational Technical Center, Board of Education, Huntsville, Alabama 35804 (free)

Magnetic Patterns of the English Language: Communications Skills Course Veritas Publications, Inc. P.O. Box 4985, Falls Church, Virginia 22044

Teaching English as a Second Language in the Kindergarten, Teaching English As a Second Language in Elementary & Secondary Schools. Center for Applied Linguistics, 1611 North Kent Street, Arlington, Virginia. 22209.

Easy Materials for the Spanish-Speaking. Committee on Reading Improvement for Adults. Adult Services Division, American Library Association, 50 E. Huron Street, Chicago, Illinois 60611 (free)

Children and Intercultural Education. Association for Childhood Education International, 3615 Wisconsin Avenue, N.W. Washington, D.C. 20016 (three part series)

Mass Remediation of Children's Reading Problems, Book-Lab, Inc. 1449 Thirty-Seventh St., Brooklyn, New York 11218 (free)

School Volunteer Programs: A Guideline. Superintendent of Public Information, Old Capitol Building, Olympia, Washington. 98504.

ABC: A Handbook for Educational Volunteers. Project Print, Building 20, Room 105, Washington Technical Institute, 4100 Connecticut Avenue, N.W., Washington, D.C. 20006. (free)

School Volunteers: What They Do and How They Do It. Citation Press, 50 West 44th St., New York, N.Y. 10036

Tutoring Tricks & Tips. National Commission on Resources for Youth, 36 West 44th St., New York, N.Y. 10036 (free)

Being a Friend to the Physically Handicapped. American Lutheran Church Women, 422 So. Fifth Street, Minneapolis, Minnesota 55415 (free)

Volunteer Handbook: Service to Shut-Ins. Los Angeles Public Library, Service to Shut Ins. Betty Gay, 5923 S. Western Avenue, Los Angeles, California 90047 (free)

Service to Shut-Ins. (Same address as above)

Recreation of the Blind Adult. American Federation for the Blind. 15 West 16th Street. New York, N.Y. 10011 (free)

FILMS . . . DRAMAS. . . . SLIDES. . . . EXHIBITS FOR EDUCATIONAL PURPOSES

Plays for Living (Scripts for plays) Family Service. Association of America, 44 East 23rd Street, New York, New York 10010 (free)

To Market, To Market. (48 color 2mm slides) free on loan. The Sperry & Hutchinson Company, Consumer Services, 2900 West Seminary Drive, Fort Worth, Texas 76133

Picture Talks on Art. Rice Museum, Rice University. Institute for the Arts, P.O. Box 1892, Houston, Texas 77001 (free)

Ethnic Art Slide Library Catalog. Ethnic American Art Slide Library, The College of Arts and Sciences, The University of Southern Alabama, Mobile, Alabama 36688

Color, Texture, Design in Space (Study Manual # 401) (Teacher's Manual # 404) The Sperry Hutchinson Company, Consumer Services, 2900 West Seminary Drive, Fort Worth, Texas 76133.

Traveling Exhibits, Traveling Exhibits Service, Smithsonian Institute, Washington, D.C. 20560 (Write for Information)

Menu Rummy (Game to learn about Nutrition) Bulletin Room, Institute of Agriculture, University of Minnesota, St. Paul, Minnesota 55101.

Narrative Guides and Slides Photograph Division, Office on Information, United States Department of Agriculture. Washington, D.C. 20250. Topics: Selecting & Buying Food for the Young Family; Improving Teenage Nutrition

Liturgy: Ministry to the Sick & Dying

Illness and Death. a complete bibliography. The Murphy Center for Liturgical Research, Notre Dame, Ind.

Community, Church and Healing. Lambourne, R.A., Darton, Longman, and Todd, London, 1963.

Creative Ministry. Henri Nouwen. Doubleday, Garden City, New York. 1971

Sacrament and Forgiveness. Palmer, Paul. Newman Press, Westminister, Maryland. 1959

What a Modern Catholic Believes About Death. Nowell, Robert. Thomas More, Chicago. 1972

Sacraments and Orthodoxy. Schemann, Alexander. Herder and Herder, New York., 1965.

On Becoming a Widow. Start, Clarissa. Concordia, St. Louis, 1968.

Portraits of Aging. Smith, Jean Louise. St. Mary's College Press, Winona, Minn., 1972.

"Healing: Sacrament or Charism?" Talley, Thomas. *Worship.* (Nov. 1972)

Death and Dying. Veatch, Robert. Claretian Publ., Chicago.

Preaching to the Sick. Yost, Charles. Priests of the Sacred Heart. Hales Corners, Wisconsin.

Death: The Final Stage of Growth. Kübler-Ross, Elisabeth. Prentice-Hall, Englewood Cliffs, N.J., 1975

Audio-visuals:

Death of a Christian. (filmstrip) Thomas Klise, Peoria, Ill.

Farewell. (16 mm film) Wm. Brown Co., Dubuque, Iowa.

How Can I Not Be Among You? (16mm film) The Eccentric Circle, P.O. Box 1418, Evanston, Illinois, 60204.

Stringbean. Mass Media Ministries. 1720 Chouteau Avenue, St. Louis, Missouri. 63103

Until I Die (by Kübler-Ross—16mm film) Video-Nursing, 2834 Central, Evanston, Illinois. 60201

Training Programs

SOS-10 *How To Plan Better Meetings and Training Programs.* National Council on the Aging, Inc. 1828 L Street, N.W. Washington, D.C. 20036

Techniques for Organizational Effectiveness. American Association of University Women, 2401 Virginia Avenue, N.W., Washington, D.C. 20037

More than 100 Ways to Sabotage a Project. Notes from a Saboteur's Handbook. Center for a Voluntary Society, 1785 Massachusetts Avenue, N.W., Washington, D.C. 20036

Uplift: What People Themselves Can Do. Project UPLIFT. Jaycees Foundation, 1800 Wisconsin Avenue, N.W., Washington, D.C. 20007 (free)

Organizing and Conducting Community Surveys. Bulletin Room, Cooperative Extension Service, Colorado State University, Fort Collins, Colorado 80521 (free)

Community Orientation Training Course: A Manual. Voluntary Action Center, United Council and Fund, P.O. Box 2688. 163 Woodlawn Terrace, Waterbury, Connecticut 06720.

Publicity

Publicity Handbook. The Sperry & Hutchinson Co., Consumer Services 2900 West Seminary Drive, Fort Worth, Texas 76133

How to Be a Communications Chairman. General Federation of Women's Clubs, Program Office, 1734 N. Street, N.W., Washington, D.C. 20036

Publicity Answers for Club Leaders. Sears Roebuck, & Company. Department 703, Public Relations, Sears Towers, Chicago, Ill. 60684. (free)

Pamphlets: How to Write & Print Them. National Public Relations Council of Health & Welfare Services, 815 Second Avenue, New York, N.Y. 10017

T.V. Spots: 100 Ideas. Modern Talking Picture Service, 4 Nevada Drive, Lake Success, New York 11040 (free)

24 Group Methods & Techniques in Adult Education. Executive Systems Corporation, Suite 300, 1750 K Street, N.W., Washington, D.C. 20006

Guide to Publicity. Materials Development Division, American Heart Association, 44 East 23rd Street, New York, N.Y. 10010 (free)